Front and back inside covers - Four panels of Sunflowers - Collection of Mary Anne Frank-Tarsi

So Italian

Traditional Recipes With My Art And Travel Notes

Paul V. Canonici

Full moon over Assisi

From my sketchbook

All I see

all I see is green water, a broad band of light green and then further out a darker green, 'til it meets the narrow strip of pinkish blue sky.

All I see are surging white caps, a little sand and rocks.

All I see is blue sky, scattered clouds, an occasional seagull gliding by.

But that's all I need to feed my innermost self and lift my soul to a place where I can be alone with my God. 5-22-02

Lobues
5-21-02

ii

For Joseph A. Canonici and Louise Gainspoletti Canonici

My brother, Joe, wrapped me in his coat and kept me warm next to his own body on cold winter mornings when we waited for the school bus. I was seven and he fifteen.

During the years that Joe and his wife, Louise, were nurturing their six children, they also nurtured our parents with tender care. At our mother's death, Louise could say she had lived in the home with our mother longer than she had lived with her own.

In their golden years, Joe has inspired us all with his loving care for his devoted Louise.

As an expression of profound gratitude and heartfelt love I dedicate this book to Joe and Louise.

6-14-04
MURANO LIGHT HOUSE

Foreword

Like a good pasta sauce, Paul Canonici is a balanced blend of flavors. Although rooted in Mississippi Delta mud, he basks in his marvelously rich Italian heritage. Constantly growing in retirement, he nurtures ties of friendship formed in his career as priest and educator. The pages of his book, "So Italian," reflect the balanced flavors that make up the author.

The heart of Italian cooking is in the home and the best way to experience Paul is in his home. My family and I like being there because in Paul's home we feel surrounded by a feast for the senses, from exciting aromas of food cooking to the visual buffet of his art collection. His book is an expression of what my family and I experience in Paul's home, a gracious expression of himself.

Paul's book is about the interests he pursues in his retirement and his interests are rooted in his philosophy of life. Paul believes that life serves us all a lemon now and then. We can bite, grimace and become sour, or we can make lemonade. Paul prefers to make lemonade, and this is his personal recipe:

Retreat to a favorite place.

Do art inspired by the place.

Cook and celebrate with friends.

Exercise the body daily.

For a healthy mind and body, thoroughly integrate all of the above with daily prayer.

It is easy to see how travel, food and art are so closely related in Paul's life. They are ingredients that, combined with exercise and prayer, evoke feelings of satisfaction, enjoyment and well-being. I'm sure this book will do the same!

Buon appetito and happy cooking.

Clark Brennan - Brennan Restaurants

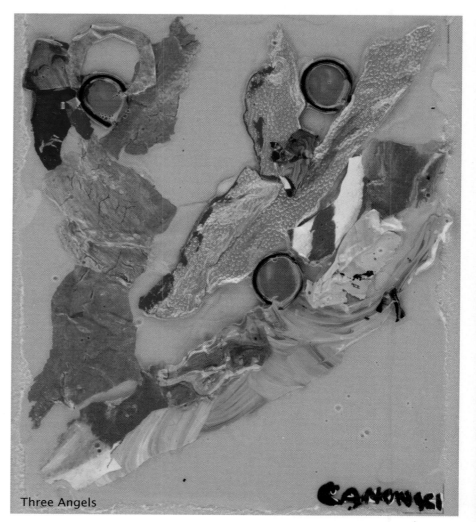

Three Angels

Acknowledgements

My parents, Alessandro Canonici and Rosa Casci Ceccacci, passed on to me our Italian heritage while they rooted me firmly in the Delta mud of their adopted country. Through the years my Italian relatives and friends shared with me their meals, recipes and food experience.

Mary Anne Frank-Tarsi has encouraged me in this project and given the project financial support.

Bob Pennebaker, Regina Burckel and Mary Pat Smith convinced me that I could do art. They and their spouses have encouraged me all the way.

Clark Brennan wrote the Foreword for this book. He, his wife, Tiffany, and their daughters, Shelby, Blair and Shayne, are my dear friends.

My friends Laurin Fields Stamm and her daughter, Lauri Stamm Collins, proofed the book and made valuable suggestions.

Hugh and Mary Dayle McCormick gave invaluable advice, especially for marketing the book.

Another friend, Jean Canizaro Enochs, also proofed the book and made a very special contribution by correcting Italian spellings.

Randall Teasley handled all technical details and designed the book. He and his wife, Susan, have been great traveling companions for me on three trips to Italy.

Pam Minninger contributed many long hours to this project typing, correcting and re-typing as she put the text of this book on her computer. She and her husband, Kerry, have been dear friends and have supported me in all my endeavors. This book would not have been possible without their assistance.

I am profoundly grateful to these and all my friends whose love and encouragement enable me daily to look beyond my limitations and reach for the stars.

Portofino

Contents

each place setting; 4 forks, spoon, embroidered napkins, wine glasses, etc --- This is service you would expect in a 5 star restaurant. The meals are being served by some of the local farmer wives -- and what a meal! Sparkling Wine all evening

Antipasta:
- Onions Carmelized in Balsamic Vinegar
- Artichoke Hearts
  Beignets

Prima Course:
  Tortolino in Broth made of Capon, Chicken, Beef
  Tortolino with Pumpkin filling
  Tortolino with Rigatto filling
  Cappaline w/ Parsley

Seconda Course:
  Roasted Rabbit, and Chicken
  Salad w/ Balsamic Vinegar
  Roasted Tomatoes in Balsamic Vinegar
  Roasted Zucchini Squash

Dessert:
  Fried Cream
  Cream Tart
  Roasted Chestnut
After Dinner Drink made of Walnut Pits.

This was an absolutely superb meal -- one of the finest the group had ever eaten!! We all rolled into bed @ 11:00.

NOV 9: MP & I over slept again today -- We awoke @ 9:30 AM -- The room were so dark with the blinds and shutters closed that we did not realize how late it was. The rest of the group was in the restaurant waiting on us -- They had already eaten --- I took a tray with sweet cake and tea to MP and then returned to the restaurant for coffee and sweet cake. Paola came by the table and talked for a while, explaining the history of the estate that has been in her family for over 250 years. When we paid our bill and checked out, she wrote everything by hand. No computer here! As we departed -- Paola gave us two bags of her homemade Almond cookies for our journey and wished us well and to come back again. Almost like a family greeting. In the van again and off to Main St deli Angeli which is a 3½ hour drive on the A1/A45 Autostrada. We decided

A visit to Villa Gaidello from the travel notes of
Bill Smith - In his memory.

vii

Introduction

My early travels covered most of Europe and South America. Attempting to take home as much as I thought possible, I kept a detailed journal and took volumes of photographs. In recent years my travels have been limited mostly to Italy, and a sketch pad and watercolors have replaced my journal and camera. All the art in this book was inspired by the Italian countryside, which somehow motivates even the amateur to pick up his pencil and paintbrush. Much is scanned from my pad. With my art and travel notes, also gleaned from my sketch pad, I have tried to give context to my collection of recipes and discussion about traditional Italian cooking.

In the average Italian home there is a ritual for preparing and serving food and for eating. Breakfast (*colazione*) is light, just coffee and bread or a roll. Lunch (*pranzo*) is at one o'clock and the entire family is expected to be present. Dinner (*cena*) is at eight o'clock in the evening, after shops close. There is very little eating between meals, although some may have a roll with coffee at mid-morning or a light snack (*merenda*) in late-afternoon.

The full meal consists of an *antipasto*, a *primo* (usually pasta), a *secondo* (main course) with *contorni* (vegetables), and a *dolce* (sweet). The *antipasto* is like an hors d'oeuvre. It is light and sets a tone for the meal. The *primo* is some kind of pasta or a related dish, like rice or soup. Every Italian expects pasta at least once daily. The *secondo* is the entrée and is served with vegetables. If there is a salad, it is served as a *contorno* with the entrée or after the entrée because it is supposed to

Venice - Flower Market

help digestion. Fruit and cheese (*frutta e formaggio*) sometimes takes the place of desserts (*dolci*).

The Italian kitchen celebrates local and seasonal products. In the Alpine regions, where grazing pastures are ample, cooks rely heavily on dairy products. The Po Valley and the region of Piamonte grow Italy's rice. They gave birth to risotto. In Calabria and other warm southern regions that have an abundance of vegetables and fruit, cooks have found myriad ways to do eggplant and tomatoes. Differing regional resources account for differences in cuisine.

Most old Italian recipes give general measurements, leaving much to the imagination of the cook. A few measurements are: *una manciatta* (a handful), *una bella manciatta* (a big handful), *un pizzico* (a pinch), *un ciuffo* (the upper part of a bunch of herbs, like the leaves in a bunch of parsley). Some Italian recipes specify measurements like *unpo* or *poco* (a little), *qualche* (a few). More often than not, herbs are listed without measurements: *rosmarino* (rosemary), *basilico* (basil). Sometimes wines are listed without giving quantities: *Marsala secco* (dry Marsala) or *vino bianco secco* (dry white wine). The amount of pasta is measured by the number of eggs used. Everyone is supposed to know how much pasta four eggs will make. My relative Marina Calderigi told me recently that she was recording her mother's recipes and they have absolutely no measurements or quantities.

Early Italian immigrants brought to America recipes for the simple foods they knew during hard times, and those are the dishes passed down to us: pasta, polenta, gnocchi, stuffed roasted chicken and *potacchio*. They brought recipes for fish dishes made from products that required no refrigeration, like *baccala* and *stocafisso*. They also brought to America the skillful art of preserving pork without refrigeration: *prosciutto*, *lonza* and sausage; and they brought the art of wine making. Italian-American cooks brought some vegetables and beans and they adopted what they found here. They brought eggplant, zucchini, fava and chickpeas. Okra was new to my mother, but she mixed it in the roasting pan with tomato halves atop eggplant halves.

Today, at least a hundred years after our people settled in America, many Italian-Americans call all pasta "macaroni" and they call pasta sauce "gravy." With the passing of time, many Italian-Americans began over-cooking pasta and using far more sauce than their Italian counterparts. Italians use just enough sauce to coat pasta.

For many Americans "pasta" means "spaghetti and meatballs." Only once have I seen meatballs (*polpette*) on the menu of an Italian restaurant, and that was not in connection with pasta. There's an endless number of pasta sauces. The only requirement for a sauce is that ingredients be fresh.

Italian recipes always use fresh garlic. You can tell when an American restaurant uses garlic powder or garlic salt; the garlic keeps coming back. My Italian relatives rarely use black pepper. They say it is hard to digest. They sometimes season with *peperoncino* (red hot pepper), but seasoning is usually very subtle.

Mixing sauces and flavors is a "no-no" for Italians. That is why they change plates for different courses. An Italian relative once told me that we Americans eat like the Chinese. He said we mix all our food in one plate. Italians use a surprising number of plates, especially at formal meals, but few homes have dishwashers. The dish rack is in a cabinet over the kitchen sink to allow dishes to drip dry.

My research focused on the traditional dishes of Italy's various regions, dishes that your parents and mine were accustomed to before coming to America. In this book I have included recipes for the classical pasta sauces and also for those quick and easy sauces thrown together by peasant women who had little time for the kitchen and little wood for the stove. I have included recipes for meats, fish and vegetable dishes that were most typical to various regions of Italy. I hope you will enjoy the recipes, my travel notes and my art as much as I enjoyed my travels and research.

Florence - Palazzo Vecchio

FLorene
PAlAzzo

Antipasti

Appetizers

The *antipasto* is the beginning of the meal and sets the tone for the meal. It is just a starter and should not be filling. It should be light, fresh and well presented. I always warn first-time visitors to Italy to pace themselves with the *antipasto* and other dishes served early in the meal, because there's plenty more food to follow.

Italians usually arrive at a host home or restaurant just in time for the meal. We Americans ask our guests to come about an hour before mealtime. In my home I like to have my antipasti out, usually in the kitchen, when my guests arrive. Whether I invite them to the kitchen or not, that's where my guests gather. I like it that way. We visit and have our *antipasti* while I finish cooking.

Salumi

One of the most common *antipasti* is an assortment of cured meats, salumi. The platter of *salumi* (*affettato misto*) contains a variety of cured meats, but always in small quantities.

Mixed Cheeses

An assortment of mixed cheeses also makes a good *antipasto*. Cheeses may be mixed with the *salumi*.

Asparagus Wrapped in *Prosciutto*

Asparagus, quantity desired, hard ends removed

Prosciutto, 1 very thin slice per stem of asparagus

Olive oil

Salt and pepper

Drizzle asparagus with olive oil. Add salt and pepper. Make sure that asparagus is oiled all over.

Spread asparagus on a baking sheet and bake at 350° for about 20 minutes. Do not overcook. Asparagus should be crunchy.

Wrap a slice of *prosciutto* around each stem of asparagus. Leave tip of asparagus exposed.

Melon and *Prosciutto*

Melon and *prosciutto* is another popular *antipasto*.

Wrap a thin slice of *prosciutto* around a small slice of melon, or drape the *prosciutto* over the melon.

Prosciutto wrapped around a small wedge of pear or around a fig also makes a good *antipasto*.

Bruschetta and Crostini

Bruschetta is a slice of firm bread toasted and seasoned with garlic and olive oil.

Just rub the hot, toasted bread with a piece of garlic and drizzle on a little olive oil. The bread can also be seasoned with a rubbing of *peperoncino* (red pepper).

Crostini are very similar to the bruschetta. The crostini consist of slices of firm bread, like baguette, toasted, brushed with olive oil and topped with just about anything - salmon, tuna, paté, seasoned mashed beans. I like to top crostini with a mixture of chopped tomato, basil and olive oil and seasoned with salt and pepper.

Vegetable Market - Senigallia

Chicken Liver Crostini

¼ cup olive oil

1 rib celery, minced

1 shallot, minced

1 large garlic clove, minced

3 tablespoons chopped parsley

½ pound chicken livers, finely chopped

¼ pound lean ground beef

1 tablespoon tomato paste

½ cup dry white wine

Salt and pepper

1 tablespoon capers, chopped

1 anchovy fillet, chopped

2 tablespoons butter

Heat olive oil in a saucepan. Add celery, shallot, garlic and parsley. Cook until soft, about 10 minutes. Add chicken livers and beef. Cook over low heat until meat is browned.

Add tomato paste, diluted in wine, raise heat and cook until wine has evaporated. Lower heat; add salt and plenty of pepper. Simmer 30 minutes. If mixture appears too dry, add a little hot water. Mix in capers and anchovy. Cook 5 minutes more.

Toast firm slices of bread. Brush with olive oil. Spread on mixture. Drizzle lightly with olive oil.

Region: Tuscany

Crostini with Sun-Dried Tomatoes

Sun-dried tomatoes, in quantity desired

Wine vinegar

Extra virgin olive oil

3 cloves garlic, cut in large pieces

Dried red hot pepper, cut in four pieces

Slices of firm bread

The day before, soak tomatoes in boiling water, just covered. Add vinegar. Soak for 2½ hours. Drain and dry tomatoes. Cut into ½-inch strips. Put tomato strips in a dish. Pour on olive oil. Distribute pieces of garlic and hot pepper. Marinate for 24 hours.

Toast bread on both sides. Drizzle generously with oil from marinade. Lay on a strip of tomato. Discard garlic and hot pepper. Drizzle again with oil from marinade.

Trout Salad

For four people:

Four medium-size trout, cleaned

2 lemons

Salt and pepper to taste

1 teaspoon parsley, chopped

2 hard-cooked eggs

Bring plenty salted water to a gentle boil. Add trout and allow to cook for 10 minutes. Gently remove trout from water. Peel and filet trout.

Place in serving dish in a single layer. Season with salt, pepper and lemon juice. Slice hard-cooked egg and spread over trout. Sprinkle with parsley. Allow to rest at room temperature for about an hour and serve.

This dish can serve as an *antipasto* or as an entrée (*secondo*).

Region: Trentino Alto Adige

Stuffed Mushrooms

Large cap mushrooms, quantity desired, cleaned with damp cloth, stems removed and reserved

Bread crumbs

Anchovy fillet

Garlic, chopped

Fresh marjoram, chopped

Pinch of nutmeg

Salt and pepper

Olive oil

Parsley, chopped

Chop mushroom stems together with bread crumbs, anchovy, garlic and marjoram. Add nutmeg, salt and pepper.

Heat olive oil and add chopped mixture. Sauté 5 minutes.

Place mushroom caps in a baking dish. Sprinkle with salt and pepper. Fill mushrooms with mixture and drizzle with olive oil. Sprinkle with parsley and bake about 15 minutes at 400°. Serve at room temperature.

Fried Squash Blossoms

Squash blossoms, unwashed, in quantity desired

For the batter:

1 egg, yolk and white separated

2 tablespoons water or white wine

1 tablespoon olive oil

Salt and pepper

2 tablespoons flour

Vegetable oil for frying

Prepare a batter consisting of the egg yolk, a little water or white wine, olive oil, salt and pepper and flour. The mixture should be rather fluid.

Allow the batter to rest for ½ hour. Beat the egg white well, until it peaks, and fold it into the batter.

Do not wash the blossoms, but remove stems. Dredge the blossoms through the batter. Shake off excess batter and fry in plenty of vegetable oil. Drain on paper towel. Serve hot and crispy.

Fried squash blossoms may serve as an *antipasto* or as a vegetable.

Fried Eggplant

Eggplant, in quantity desired, peeled and cut lengthwise into thin slices

For batter: 1 egg, lightly beaten

Salt and pepper

Bread crumbs for dredging

Beat egg lightly and add a little salt and pepper. Dredge the eggplant slices through the egg and then through fine bread crumbs. The batter used for zucchini blossoms may be used for eggplants.

Fry the eggplant in plenty of vegetable oil. Drain on paper towels.

Fried eggplant may be used as an *antipasto* or as a vegetable dish.

Urbino

CANONICI

Tasty Crepes

4 eggs, separated

2 cups milk

4 tablespoons flour

3 anchovy fillets, chopped finely and mashed

1 tablespoon parsley, finely chopped

Salt and pepper

Olive oil

Lightly beat the egg yolks. Add salt, pepper and flour. Mix well. Combine parsley and anchovy. Mash into a paste and add to egg mixture. Pour the combined mixture into the milk a little at a time while constantly mixing.

Beat the egg whites until they peak. Carefully fold the egg whites into the milk mixture.

Heat a crepe pan and coat the inside with olive oil. For each crepe pour into the pan just enough batter to lightly coat the bottom of the pan. Crepes will cook quickly.

Roll each crepe as it is taken from the pan and place on a warm platter. Keep crepes warm. Garnish the crepes with sprigs of parsley and serve.

Region: Trentino Alto Adige

Cheese Croquettes

⅔ cup all-purpose flour

⅔ pound Fontina cheese, diced

6 tablespoons butter

1 cup milk

2 egg yolks

1 whole egg for dredging

Salt and pepper to taste

Pinch of nutmeg

Bread crumbs for dredging

Oil for frying

Combine the flour, Fontina, milk, butter, salt, pepper and nutmeg. Stir and cook over moderate heat. Bring to a boil, stirring constantly. When the boil begins, there should be a smooth dense consistency.

Remove from heat and stir in egg yolks. Pour the mixture into a bowl and allow to cool.

Form cheese balls about the size of ping-pong balls. Dredge the balls through egg and then through the bread crumbs. Fry in hot oil and serve immediately.

Region: Valle d'Aosta

Apennine Mountains

Lady in the window

Sicilian Rice Balls (Arancini)

1½ cups rice, cooked *al dente* according to instructions

1 cup Pecorino cheese, grated (or Parmesan)

2 eggs, plus 1 egg for dredging

1 teaspoon saffron, diluted in very little warm water

¼ pound mozzarella cheese, diced

3 tablespoons butter

Flour for dredging

Bread crumbs for dredging

Olive oil or Crisco (*Strutto*) for frying

Combine cooked rice, Pecorino, 2 slightly beaten eggs and saffron. Mix well and allow to rest 15 minutes. Take a large spoonful of mixture into the palm of your left hand, and with your right hand, form a small cup with the mixture. Place a little butter and three or four cubes of mozzarella in the cup. Close the cup with another spoonful of mixture and roll the contents into a ball.

Roll the *arancini* (little oranges) in the beaten egg, then in the flour and finally in the bread crumbs. Fry in a deep pan with plenty of oil or Crisco. Allow the *arancini* to drain on a paper towel.

Fried Bean Balls

1 pound White Northern beans

1 onion

1 rib celery

2 stems cloves, stuck in onion

3 eggs, separated

1 cup bread crumbs

3 tablespoons Parmesan cheese

Vegetable oil for frying

Soak beans overnight. Cook beans with the whole onion, celery, cloves and salt. Cook until very tender. Drain beans. Remove onion, celery and cloves. Pass beans through a ricer or puree in blender.

Combine beans, the three egg yolks, Parmesan, sufficient bread crumbs to form a thick, manageable consistency, and a pinch of salt if necessary. Mix well.

Shape mixture into bean balls the size of golf balls. Dredge the bean balls in lightly beaten egg whites and then in bread crumbs. Fry the bean balls in plenty of hot oil. Drain the balls on a paper towel and serve.

These go well with a mixed salad or as an *antipasto*.

Region: Trentino Alto Adige

Beans with Wine

1 pound Borlotti beans (If Borlotti beans are not available, use kidney beans.)

1 whole onion

⅓ pound speck or 5 thick slices lean bacon

4 tablespoons butter

1 tablespoon flour

2 cups red wine

Salt and pepper to taste

Soak beans overnight. Put beans in a saucepan with the whole onion and unchopped speck/bacon. Pour in wine and add water to 1½ inches above the beans. Add salt to taste and cook until beans are tender but not mushy.

When the beans are cooked, remove the onion and speck/bacon. Dice the speck/bacon and allow it to sauté in the butter with the flour for 10 minutes. Add the resulting sauce to the beans; mix and cook over low heat for an additional 10 minutes.

Check the beans while they are cooking. If more liquid is needed, add a little water.

Tuscany - Villa among sunflowers

Florence - Duomo

My Search For Traditional Italian Cuisine

Rome - Colosseum

Nostalgia for the Italy my parents left in the early nineteen-hundreds pushes me to search out restaurants that do the traditional Italian cuisine. In my opinion, some of Italy's most prestigious restaurants have become ultra-modern in their cooking styles and presentations. I have no complaint with the quality of food in those restaurants. Their food and presentations are exquisite, but it's not the traditional Italian cuisine. In Italy I like to eat traditional Italian food. I like to hear Italian music; and I like Italian writing on T-shirts. It was June, 1972, my first trip to Italy and my first time in Rome. I thought I should pinch myself to see if it was true. At a Roman restaurant that first evening I told the waiter I wanted a typical Italian meal, so Italian I would know I was really in Italy. He responded, *"Qui si mangia Romano."* (Here one eats Roman). That was my first encounter with Italian regional pride. As a first dish he recommended a Roman favorite, *pasta alla carbonara* (p.19).

On a subsequent visit to Rome I discovered Mario's Restaurant. It's near the Spanish Steps. There is nothing really exciting about the outside, just a neon sign overhead and the usual menu with prices at the entrance, but once you open the door to Mario's Restaurant, the aromas of cooking foods draw you in. The restaurant's walls are covered with photos of Mario and his distinguished guests, movie stars and other well-knowns from everywhere. You can't miss Mario with his bushy black eyebrows. He used to make the rounds greeting guests, and now and then gave away copies of his booklet containing something about himself and his restaurant, a few of his recipes and pictures of himself with celebrated guests. I haven't seen Mario on recent visits. He has problems with his knees, so he stays in his apartment upstairs. Maria, his wife, comes in early to get Mario's dinner and after she and Mario have finished their dinner, she comes back to supervise the restaurant's operations from the elevated nook toward the back of the main dining room and just outside the kitchen.

For me, the restaurant would not be Mario's without Roberto, the head waiter. He was there on my first visit. His service won my heart and continues to draw me back to the restaurant. There were five in my party the evening of that first visit. We studied the menu and chatted about what to order. About the time we were ready to order, Roberto said, *"Ci penso io."* (I will decide). He made an excellent choice. Among several *antipasti* there was Mario's Beans, a specialty of the house (p.111). We sampled three different pastas. I especially liked the pasta with a broccoli sauce. Roberto brought at least two meats. I liked the wild boar (*cinghiale*) best. There was an assortment of desserts, several of Maria's tarts (p.142-43). Finally Roberto brought after-dinner drinks.

Roberto will decide my menu whenever I go to Mario's, and when my friends ask about a restaurant in Rome, I always give Mario's Restaurant as the first choice. I tell them to ask for Roberto. "Tell him you want to be served the way he serves me."

The Marche region - Shrine of Loreto

With David
Trigiani
Loreto
May 20/00

Primi-First Courses

- Homemade Pasta
- The Classic Pasta Sauces
- Quick and Easy Pasta Sauces
- Easy Pasta Sauces – No Cooking
- Tortellini
- Ravioli
- Lasagna
- Gnocchi
- Risotto
- Polenta
- Broths, Minestras and Soups

Homemade Pasta

Many Italian cooks buy "homemade" pasta. " Pasta *All'uovo*" shops are easily accessible and pasta can be bought in all forms. Most shops will cut pasta to the customer's liking on the spot. Generally shops roll out dough and cut pasta with a machine but there are still those who do the entire process by hand.

My mother and her contemporaries did the entire pasta process by hand. I use a hand cranked pasta machine but I'm told that machine-made pasta is not as good as the one made completely by hand. Rolling out dough by hand is almost a lost art. Jeannie Malatesta Roberts and Eva Balducci Gratafiori, Clarksdale, MS, are the only Mississippians I know who still roll out dough and cut pasta completely by hand.

Jeannie has her grandmother's rolling pin, an unpainted broom handle. Most homes had a special board for rolling out dough and cutting pasta but a clean counter surface will work.

The quantity of pasta is always measured by the number of eggs used. Once the quantity of eggs and other liquids are designated, flour is added and kneaded in until the desired consistency is obtained. The following is Jeannie Malatesta Roberts' recipe for "4 eggs of pasta" which should make six generous servings.

4 Eggs of Pasta

3½ **cups all purpose flour. Some use equal quantities of flour and semolina.**

4 eggs

1 tablespoon olive oil

1 or 2 tablespoons water

1 generous pinch salt

Mound the flour on a kneading board or clean counter. Make a well in the flour and add eggs, oil, water and salt. With a fork break the egg yolks and slowly incorporate the flour until you can work the dough with your hands. Work the dough until you obtain a velvety consistency. The dough should be smooth and elastic. If it is still sticky add a little flour. If it is too dry add a few drops of water. It is not necessary to use all the flour. Keep the working surface floured. Wrap the dough in plastic wrap and allow it to rest at room temperature for about 30 minutes.

With a rolling pin flatten out the dough and begin to work it into a sheet (*sfoglia*). When the desired thinness is obtained, fold the large sheet of dough back and forth to form a stack of dough about 2 ½ inches wide. Then cut the dough into pasta the width desired. After every five or six cuttings, toss the cut pasta onto the working surface to separate the strands. The sheet of pasta may be used for any type of pasta including lasagna and pastas with a filling.

Cook the pasta in plenty salted water. Handmade pasta cooks quickly, just two or three minutes.

The dough can be started in a mixer or food processor and finished by hand. Adjust flour or moisture to obtain the desired consistency. Also, the dough may be rolled out and cut with a hand cranked machine. If the machine is used, cut off pieces of dough as you roll and keep the remainder wrapped in plastic to keep it from drying out. Clean your pasta machine with a dry cloth. Never apply water to your machine.

Florence - Ponte Vecchio

Primi 15

The Classic Pasta Sauces

Some pasta sauces are considered classic because they may be found on menus in all regions of Italy. The classics have been around a long time and all have variations according to region, cook and taste. Some of the classics were in existence before the arrival of the tomato in Italy. Consequently, the original recipes did not contain tomato. Every cook is free to adjust the classics, or any other recipes, to suit personal taste. That is why most Italian recipes do not prescribe precise quantities for herbs and other seasonings.

Basic Tomato Sauce

1 can (28 oz.) diced tomatoes or puree

1 onion, chopped

2 celery stalks, chopped

1 carrot, finely chopped

3 tablespoons olive oil

2 tablespoons basil, chopped

Heat oil in saucepan. Add onion, celery and carrot. Cook over low heat for 15 minutes.

Add tomatoes and cook over medium heat 30 minutes. Add basil and remove from heat.

The basic sauce may be frozen and used as needed.

Aglio, Olio and Peperoncino (garlic, olive oil and hot pepper)

The classic *aglio, olio* and *peperoncino* has a number of variations and there are different ways of treating the ingredients. For instance, the garlic cloves may be used whole or in large pieces and removed when the oil is seasoned. Whether the garlic is removed or not, it should not be allowed to cook until dark brown. Another ingredient that may be used in different ways is the *peperoncino* (hot pepper). The absolute classic requires the *peperoncino* to be cut into three or four pieces and removed after the oil is seasoned. It is absolutely important to cut the pepper. My friend J.W. is wild about *Aglio, Olio* and *Peperoncino*. One day he decided to make some for himself. Having had little cooking experience he failed to cut the pepper and it exploded in the hot oil filling his house with a burning hot vapor. Pepper flakes or ground red pepper may be used instead of the whole cut pepper. I like to use red pepper flakes. The *Aglio, Olio* and *Peperoncino* is one of the quickest and easiest pasta sauces, and a favorite with many Italians.

Olive oil, just enough to coat pasta

3 cloves garlic, minced if it is to remain in the sauce, otherwise whole or cut into large pieces

Red pepper or pepper flakes to taste (be sure to cut the red pepper)

Heat oil in a skillet. Add garlic and red pepper. If the garlic and/or the red pepper will be removed, remove before the garlic turns brown. Cook pasta *al dente* in plenty of salted water. Pour hot pasta into pan with sauce. Toss and serve. Parmesan or Pecorino may be sprinkled on the pasta or served on the side. Also, before tossing, a couple of spoonfuls of the cooking water may be added to the pasta and sauce.

ARENA-VERONA

Canonici

Verona - Roman arena

Arrabbiata - Prepared in an Angry Mood

Alla Arrabbiata means "in an angry way." It is quite possible that the sauce got its name when some Italian housewife angrily threw together a quick sauce with a lot of hot pepper, with no more effort than necessary, to feed her hungry husband. The classic way to serve the sauce is with penne, but it is also good with other types of pasta.

Olive Oil

2 cloves garlic, minced

½ cup dry white wine

1 small can diced tomatoes

Pepper flakes to taste. Remember that hot pepper is the distinguishing ingredient of this sauce.

Salt and pepper to taste

Tablespoon of basil leaves, chopped

Tablespoon of parsley, chopped

Heat olive oil in skillet and sauté garlic until light golden.

Add wine and allow to evaporate. Then add tomatoes, pepper flakes, salt and pepper.

Cook over low heat for 30 minutes, adding a little warm water to maintain a dense, flowing, sauce.

Remove from heat. Stir in basil and parsley. Drain pasta, pour it into skillet with the sauce. Toss and serve.

Siena - Arched Alley

Bolognese (meat sauce)

Very few Italian dishes have one set recipe. Different regions and different families have their own way of doing dishes that go by the same name. Consequently, there is no one way to do Bolognese Sauce. This is the most basic recipe.

½ - ¾ pound lean beef, coarsely ground

4 tablespoons butter

1 onion, chopped

1 stick celery, chopped

1 carrot, chopped

Parsley, chopped

Thyme, leaves only

2 bay leaves

2 pieces clove

Salt and pepper to taste

Stock

Optional: Cup of red wine

1 small can diced tomatoes

1 tablespoon of flour

Parmesan cheese

Heat butter in a tall skillet or a saucepan. Add onion, celery, carrot and meat. When the meat begins to brown, add a little stock and continue adding from time to time so the bottom of the pan always has some liquid. At this time you may also add a cup of red wine. Allow the wine to evaporate before adding more stock. After the wine has evaporated, tomatoes may be added. Also, a sprinkling of flour may be added. Bolognese with tomatoes is more common than without.

Add parsley, thyme, bay leaves, cloves, salt and pepper. Lower heat and cook, covered, for one hour or more.

Serve grated Parmesan on the side.

Carbonara

Carbonara sauce is quick and easy. It is used with any long pasta. Prepare the sauce while the pasta is cooking, but be sure to have all the ingredients ready, oil heated in a skillet large enough to hold the cooked pasta, butter melted.

½ cup chopped *pancetta* or lean bacon

3 tablespoons butter

1 tablespoon olive oil

4 eggs, one for each person, my friends use just the yolks

Grated Pecorino. If Pecorino is not available use Parmesan

2 tablespoons heavy cream - some recipes do not require cream

Pepper

While the pasta is cooking, brown pancetta/bacon in olive oil, using a skillet large enough to hold cooked pasta. In a small bowl mix melted butter, eggs (or yolks only), ½ cup grated cheese, cream and pepper.

When pasta is cooked *al dente*, drain well and put in pan with pancetta/bacon. Toss well, pour on egg mixture and toss over low heat for just a moment.

Serve with more grated cheese on the side.

Amalfi

Marinara

Marinara is one of the sweetest tomato sauces. The secret for its sweetness is that it is cooked for a very short time.

4 tablespoons olive oil

1 can (28 oz.) tomatoes

2/3 cup black olives, chopped coarsely

2 cloves garlic, sliced thinly

2 tablespoons capers, chopped if large

A little salt

6 basil leaves

Optional: pepper flakes

Mix all ingredients and allow to rest for at least 1 hour.

Put mixture in saucepan and cook over moderate heat until sauce becomes somewhat dense, about 30 minutes.

This sauce is used preferably with long pasta like spaghetti, vermicelli and linguine.

Senigallia - Vegetable Market

Alla Matriciana

The pasta sauce Alla Matriciana originated in the village of Amatrice, from which it gets its name. It is a popular sauce in Rome and in the entire regions of Lazio and Abruzzo. Being an ancient recipe, the sauce was in existence before the tomato was brought to Europe from the Americas. Today the recipe usually contains some tomatoes. The sauce Alla Matriciana is most often used with Bucatini, the long pasta that has a tiny hole throughout its length. It can be used with other types of pasta as well.

1/2 cup chopped *pancetta* or lean bacon

2 tablespoons olive oil

1/2 chopped onion

3/4 cup dry white wine

4 tablespoons tomato sauce or 1 cup fresh tomatoes, chopped

Red pepper flakes

Salt

Grated Pecorino cheese

Cook bacon in oil until it becomes slightly brown. Add onion and cook until it is lightly golden. Add wine and allow to evaporate over medium heat.

Add tomato sauce/tomatoes and red pepper flakes and cook 3 minutes.

Drain pasta and put hot pasta in pan with sauce. Toss.

Sprinkle generously with Pecorino cheese. Parmesan may be substituted for Pecorino.

Sunflower in vase

Alla Puttanesca

Translated literally, alla puttanesca means "whore style." The sauce may have this name because the aroma was supposed to attract men walking by "the house".

   4 tablespoons olive oil

   3 cloves garlic, chopped

   1 *Peperoncino*, sliced into 3 or 4 pieces

   1 can (28 oz.) tomatoes, mashed or 1 pound fresh tomatoes

   1 heaping tablespoon capers

   ½ can, or more, black olives, sliced

   1 tablespoon dried oregano

   6 anchovy fillets, chopped

   ⅓ cup parsley, chopped

Heat oil in saucepan. Add garlic and *Peperoncino*. Cook slightly (*Peperoncino* may be removed before serving). Add tomatoes, capers, olives, and oregano. Bring to a boil and cook about 5 minutes. Add anchovies. Cook about 10 minutes. Add parsley. Stir and cook three minutes more. Toss with pasta cooked *al dente*.

An Italian-American Classic – Spaghetti and Meatballs

For many Italian-Americans, pasta means spaghetti and meatballs. On our first visit to Italy we are surprised not to find meatballs on the menus of Italian restaurants and on tables of Italian homes. I asked 95-year-old Cousin Vanda whether she was familiar with meatballs (*polpette*). She said that during really hard times some Italians mixed ground or chopped leftovers with breadcrumbs and formed little balls that they cooked with a tomato sauce. I think meatballs speak to us about our Italian-American history. Most of our immigrant ancestors were extremely poor. They brought to America the simple peasant recipes they knew. On the other hand, Italians shied away from meatballs because they preferred to forget the hard times.

Meatballs and Tomato Sauce, Shaw Style

I grew up in St. Francis of Assisi Parish, Shaw, Mississippi. When the parish has a spaghetti supper, families are asked to make meatballs and sauce. The following is the recipe assigned to each family. The recipe is for a large quantity of sauce.

Meatballs (50)

5½ lb. ground chuck

10 slices dry bread, crumbled

1 cup onion, chopped

3 tablespoons fresh or 2 tablespoons dried parsley

10 large or 13 medium eggs, beaten

1¾ cups grated Parmesan cheese

¾ cup chopped celery

4 cloves garlic, minced

Salt and pepper to taste

Mix meat, crumbs, cheese, onions, parsley, garlic, salt and pepper. Add eggs and mix well again. Form mixture into firm balls; fry in ½ cup of oil until slightly brown, turning to brown on all sides.

Sauce

½ lb. ground chuck

10 cans tomato paste (small)

1 tablespoon sugar

2 cloves garlic, minced

¾ cup celery

Salt and pepper to taste

1 small onion

5 cans tomato sauce (small)

12 – 13 cups water

1½ tablespoons fresh or 1½ teaspoons dry parsley

1½ teaspoons oregano

Place chopped onion, celery, parsley, salt, and pepper in a 6 to 8 quart pot. Add ½ cup oil (used when frying meatballs), and sauté slightly. Add meat and garlic; brown. Add tomato paste, 3 cups water, and tomato sauce. Add remaining water. Add sugar; bring to a boil, stirring constantly. Cook slowly for 30 minutes. Slowly drop in the slightly browned meatballs, and simmer for 1½ hours, stirring occasionally, so that the sauce will not stick.

Mrs. Lisa Olmi's Meat Balls

Lisa Olmi lived in Shaw, MS. She died well into her 90's. I loved her dearly and I know she loved me.

Meat balls

2 tablespoons chopped parsley

½ medium onion, chopped

2 tablespoons chopped celery

2 garlic cloves, chopped

1 lb. ground beef

2 tablespoons Parmesan cheese

½ cup moistened bread crumbs

Salt and pepper to taste

Mix all ingredients. Quantities of ingredients are approximate. Form meat balls and arrange on lightly oiled cookie sheet. Brown in oven preheated to about 350°. Then carefully arrange in saucepan and cover with sauce. Simmer 45 minutes to 1 hour.

Sauce

½ cup olive oil

2 tablespoons chopped parsley

½ medium onion, chopped

2 tablespoons chopped celery

2 garlic cloves, chopped

Meat for seasoning (2 or 3 chicken pieces or steak strips or ground beef)

28 oz. can tomato sauce (for 1 lb. of pasta 16 oz. is adequate)

1 tablespoon tomato paste

Salt and pepper to taste

1 teaspoon sugar

Country Villa

Heat oil. Simmer parsley, onion, celery, and garlic about 10 minutes. Add meat and brown. Add tomato sauce and tomato paste. Finally add salt, pepper and sugar. Simmer 1½ to 2 hours. It may be necessary to add a little water. If chicken or steak is used, remove before serving. Toss with pasta cooked *al dente* in plenty of salted water.

Traditional Italian Cuisine in Florence

My favorite restaurant in Florence is La Galleria. It's just a few yards across the Ponte Vecchio on the Pitti Palace Museum side of the Arno River. Once you've crossed the Ponte Vecchio, continue straight ahead. On your right you will see an arcade, and under the arcade there's a sign, "La Galleria." It is not a large restaurant, but there is additional eating space outside under the arcade.

The food at La Galleria is good and reasonably priced. What I find special about the restaurant are the owners, Rita and Pino. They are always there, either in the kitchen or waiting tables. On one of my visits Rita took me to the kitchen to show how she makes a delicious cream sauce for ravioli. She melts butter in a skillet and pours in about a cup of *panna*, Italian cooking cream. Then she adds a half cup of soaked porcini mushrooms and a cup of cooked green peas. She gives the sauce a simple stir and adds her cooked ravioli. That's simple enough and it's one of my favorites.

Florence - Ponte Vecchio

Florence from Ponte Trinita

1/5/99
Florence from
Ponte Trinita

Quick and Easy Pasta Sauces

Graziella's Pasta Sauce with Nuts

8 anchovy fillets, finely chopped, divided

4 cloves garlic, finely chopped

1/4 cup chopped parsley, divided

1/4 cup chopped basil, divided

3/4 cup chopped walnuts

1 small can diced tomatoes

Olive oil

Red pepper flakes to taste

Parmesan cheese

In a medium-size skillet sauté the garlic and 4 anchovies for about 2 minutes. Do not allow garlic to brown. Add tomatoes, half the parsley and half the basil. Cook for an additional 10 minutes.

Remove from heat. Add remaining chopped anchovy, parsley and basil. Drizzle with olive oil. Add red pepper flakes and cheese. Toss and serve.

Simple Tomato Sauce - Salsa al Pomodoro

A popular sauce on Italian menus is *Salsa al Pomodoro* or Tomato Sauce. Sometimes it is called *Pomodoro e Basilico*, Tomato and Basil.

1 (28-ounce) can tomatoes, drained, preferably Roma tomatoes because they have less liquid

6 tablespoons olive oil

Salt

8 or 10 leaves basil

Grated Parmesan or Pecorino cheese

In a saucepan heat the olive oil. Add tomatoes and stir.

Add salt and 8 or 10 leaves of basil. Do not wash basil, but clean with a lightly dampened cloth. Cook for 10 minutes.

Serve over hot pasta with Parmesan or Pecorino on the side.

Thyme or parsley may be used with the basil. A pinch of red pepper flakes will add a little bite to the sauce.

Sauce with Roasted Peppers and Tomatoes

6 tablespoons olive oil

2 or 3 garlic cloves

1 can (14.5 ounces) tomatoes, mashed

2 red or yellow peppers, roasted, peeled, and cut in strips

1 or 2 tablespoons capers

Salt and pepper to taste

1/4 to 1/2 cup chopped Italian parsley

Parmesan or Pecorino cheese

Roast peppers under broiler until skin is mostly black. Put in brown paper bag to cool and then peel. Clean and cut into strips.

Heat oil over medium heat. Add garlic and cook until light golden. Remove garlic. Add mashed tomatoes. When tomatoes begin to simmer, add pepper strips. Stir and add capers, salt and pepper. Finally add parsley and immediately stir into pasta cooked *al dente*.

Serve cheese on the side.

Farm House   Canonic

Sauce with Zucchini and Tomatoes

3 zucchini, diced

4 Roma tomatoes, diced

1 onion, thinly sliced, or 2 cloves garlic, finely chopped

4 tablespoons olive oil

Chopped basil

Salt and pepper

In a saucepan or skillet, heat oil and cook onion or garlic until very lightly golden.

Add zucchini. Stir and cook for 2 minutes. Then add tomatoes. Add salt, pepper and basil. Cook until zucchini become tender.

Pour sauce over pasta. Toss and serve.

Pasta Sauce with Asparagus

Gioachino and Madalena Mosci live in Ostra, Province of Ancona, about fifteen miles from the Adriatic Coast. They have a home in town where they live during the winter months and an old farmhouse just out of town near the Ostra cemetery. They stay at the farmhouse from late spring until early fall. Eighteen generations of the Mosci family have lived in the old house, remodeled except for one room that used to be the *magazzino*, the room where grain and other farm supplies were once stored. The unspoiled little room has doors less than six feet tall, causing one to wonder whether people were shorter eighteen generations ago.

The Moscis do all of their entertaining at the old farmhouse, and meals are often served outside on a patio in front of the house. To the back and side of the house there's a vineyard and rows of olive trees, some several generations old. There are also various fruit trees, like apricots and cherries. Here and there you can see clumps of rose bushes. Roses seem to bloom all year long in Italy, and they're everywhere. For one meal that we had outside, Madalena had a pasta sauce with asparagus. It's a simple recipe and delicious, served on *tagliatelle*.

1/4 cup olive oil

2 cups asparagus, diced (preferably very small asparagus. If the asparagus is larger, it is cut lengthwise and then diced) - for a good presentation leave the tips intact

1½ cups *pancetta* or lean bacon

2 egg yolks, beaten lightly

Salt to taste

Grated Parmesan

In a skillet heat olive oil. Add *pancetta*/bacon and cook about 2 minutes. Then add asparagus and sauté over low heat until asparagus is tender; salt to taste. Drain cooked pasta and put it in pan with asparagus. Add beaten egg and toss well. Serve with cheese on the side.

Liguria - S. Margherita

Sauce with Sun-Dried Tomatoes

⅔ cup sun-dried tomatoes in oil, chopped

Small can (14 oz.) diced tomatoes or tomato puree

4 tablespoons olive oil

½ onion, chopped

1 rib celery, chopped

Pepper

Heat oil in skillet and cook onion until lightly golden. Add celery and sun-dried tomatoes. Cook about 5 minutes. Add tomatoes.

If sauce appears too dense, add a cup of hot water or stock. Cook about 15 or 20 minutes, adding water if necessary. Sauce should be dense but fluid. Add pepper to taste, stir and toss with pasta.

This recipe does not require salt because sun-dried tomatoes are already salted.

Penne with Gremolata

Gremolata is a combination of parsley, lemon rind, and garlic. The pasta I recommend is penne.

1 cup packed fresh parsley, finely chopped

1 teaspoon grated lemon rind

1 garlic clove, minced

3 tablespoons extra virgin olive oil, divided

1 can (14 ounces) plum tomatoes, chopped

3 tablespoons fresh basil, chopped

1 pound penne, cooked *al dente* in plenty of salted water

Combine parsley, lemon rind, and garlic and set aside. I chop all these together in food chopper. Heat about 1½ tablespoons oil in small saucepan over medium heat. Add tomatoes, bring to a boil and cook about 10 minutes. Stir in basil.

Stir about 1 or 2 tablespoons oil into cooked pasta. Toss well. Add parsley mixture and tomatoes. Toss gently to coat.

Serve immediately.

Pasta Sauce with Figs

It is very important that figs not be overcooked. It is also important to make the sauce just before applying it to the pasta. The sauce is best with tagliatelle and tagliarini.

8 tablespoons unsalted butter

Zest of 1 lemon

12 large figs (cut into 6 or 8 parts) or 20 small figs (halved or cut into 3 or 4 parts), peeled

Red pepper flakes, about a teaspoon

½ teaspoon black pepper

¾ cup heavy cream

Parmesan cheese

Salt to taste

Melt the butter in a large skillet over medium heat just before pasta is removed from heat.

When the pasta is poured into the colander to drain, turn heat under skillet to high and add lemon zest. Cook about 30 seconds. Add figs and both peppers. Cook 1 minute, stirring figs with wooden spoon.

Put pasta in the skillet with figs, pour on cream, toss quickly and check for salt. Transfer pasta to a warm serving bowl.

Amalfi

Pasta with Ham & Mushrooms

1 cup ham, diced

2 cups mushrooms, sliced. 1 cup chopped celery may be substituted for mushrooms

1 onion, chopped

2 tablespoons butter

1 cup dry Marsala

Salt, pepper and dash of nutmeg

Grated Parmesan

Optional: 1 cup tomato and 1 clove garlic, chopped. 1 cup of chopped celery may be substituted for mushrooms

Cook onion in butter until lightly golden. Add mushrooms and cook about 5 minutes. Then add ham and cook about 5 minutes more, stirring frequently.

Add wine and allow it to evaporate. Add dash of nutmeg, salt and pepper. Add about ⅓ cup of water and cook additional 10 minutes.

Apply sauce to pasta, toss and serve. Serve grated cheese on the side.

Chopped garlic may be added with the onion. Tomatoes may be added after Marsala.

Amalfi

Vernazza - Cinque Terre

Mozzarella, Bacon & Tomato Sauce

4 or 5 slices *pancetta* or lean bacon, diced

1/2 cup mozzarella, julienned

1/3+ cup olive oil, sufficient to coat pasta

2 tablespoons butter

2 cloves garlic, minced

5 Roma tomatoes, seeded, excess liquid squeezed out, and finely chopped

1/2 cup pitted black olives, chopped

2 tablespoons parsley, chopped

Salt and Tabasco to taste

1/2 cup grated Parmesan

Heat pan over moderate flame. Add oil, butter and garlic. When garlic is lightly golden, add tomatoes (canned, diced tomatoes may be used) and parsley. Add salt and cook for about ten minutes. In the meantime, in a separate pan, brown the pancetta/bacon with a little oil. Drain the pancetta of excess grease and add to tomato sauce. Add the chopped olives and Tabasco (red pepper flakes may be substituted).

Drain cooked pasta well and add to pan with sauce and toss gently. Remove from heat and spread diced mozzarella over pasta. Sprinkle with Parmesan.

Toss gently again and serve.

Adriatic Sea - fishing camp

Lina's Eggplant and Swordfish Sauce

2 small eggplants, peeled and diced

1 pound swordfish, cut in one-inch pieces

1 onion, chopped

Olive oil for frying

1 1/2 cups tomatoes, diced

1 teaspoon dry mustard

Salt and pepper

2 tablespoons butter

Fry eggplant and swordfish separately and put aside, keep warm.

Sauté onion. Add diced tomatoes. Cook about 10 minutes. Then add eggplant and swordfish, mustard, salt and pepper. Mix and heat through.

Drain pasta and toss with butter. Add sauce, toss and serve.

Region: Sicily

Sauce with Tuna, Tomatoes and Green Peas

2 tablespoons olive oil

2 tablespoons butter

2 cloves garlic, chopped

1 can (14 oz.) diced tomatoes

1 tablespoon capers

1½ cups green peas

1 can of tuna in oil, drained,

About ½ cup chopped parsley

Salt and pepper to taste

Heat oil and butter in saucepan. Add garlic and sauté until garlic is slightly golden. Add tomatoes, capers and peas. Cook about 4 minutes.

Add drained tuna, chopped parsley, salt and pepper. Cook additional 3 minutes or until peas are cooked.

Pour over pasta, toss gently and serve.

This sauce can be made without either tomatoes or green peas. In such a case, you may also eliminate the butter but add more oil.

Clam Sauce

½ cup olive oil

½ medium onion, chopped

2 or 3 cloves garlic, finely chopped

1 cup basil leaves, finely chopped

1 small can or 2 cups diced tomatoes

1 can (10 oz.) baby clams, reserve liquid

Pepper to taste

In saucepan, heat oil and cook onion until very light golden. Add mixture of chopped garlic and basil leaves. Stir well over heat.

Add tomatoes and cook until excess liquid is evaporated. Then add liquid from clams and allow to cook until some of the liquid is evaporated (about 15 minutes). Add clams and cook about 1 minute (or less).

Add freshly ground pepper to taste. Pour over pasta and stir. Reserve a little sauce to top of pasta for presentation.

A Surprise in Emilia Romagna

Italy is full of surprises. On a trip with the Burckels and the Smiths, we discovered a treasure. It was late afternoon and having driven the Autostrada all the way from the Alps north of Milan, we were ready for a good dinner and a comfortable bed. I had heard about a farmhouse called Villa Gaidello in the vicinity of Castelfranco in Emilia, north of Bologna and just south of Modena, so we decided to check it out. We turned off of the Autostrada south of Modena and, taking a rural road, made our way to Castelfranco. After three stops for directions we found Villa Gaidello, an *agriturismo* owned and managed by Paola Bini. The farm had belonged to Paola's grandmother. An *agriturismo* is a restaurant, usually with hotel accommodations, located in a rural setting. The *agriturismo* is most often family operated, and it serves meals prepared from local products. You can find *agriturismi* (plural for *agriturismo*) all over Italy's countryside.

Castlefranco is rural. Villa Gaidello is country. We rang the bell at the gate and a dark-complected man let us in and escorted us to the reception room in the main building, which houses the kitchen and dining areas. Paola Bini, a charming lady with white hair and wear-

Villa Gaidello

ing jeans, greeted us and proceeded immediately to serve us her local sparkling wine and homemade almond cookies. Franco then helped us with our luggage and showed us to our rooms, which were in three separate buildings on the grounds.

I was in the building that was once the grandmother's horse stable. In fact, there was a concrete feeding trough in my bedroom. My traveling companions were impressed with the 18th century antiques.

When we had checked into our rooms, Paola gave us a tour of her kitchen, where local farm women do the cooking and serving. One lady was making pumpkin tortellini, a specialty of the house. Paola asked the lady to show us how she makes the tortellini, and the lady said in Italian, "I'll show them. Then get them out of here." Paola smiled and pointed toward me, "He understands everything." The lady responded, "I know," and she continued working with her tortellini.

On the stove there was a huge pot, about 20 gallons or so. It was the largest cooking pot I had ever seen. Paola said that was stock in the making for the "*tortellini in brodo*," It contained beef, capon and turkey, and would cook for fourteen hours. In addition to meats, the stock contained celery, carrots, onion, bay leaf, parsley and garlic. For everyday

Tuscany - Villa among the olives

Primi 35

use in homes, one meat alone -- chicken, turkey or beef -- is quite adequate for a good stock.

Stock, or broth as I've always called it, has multiple uses in the Italian home. It is used in soups, sauces, stews and sautés. I doubt that any ethnic cuisine uses stock in as many ways as the Italian. That is why Italian markets carry bouillon cubes (*dadi*) in every imaginable flavor and Italian cooks use them when they need stock in a hurry. The traditional *primo* for Christmas and holidays is *tortellini in brodo*, tortellini in broth. There's hardly anything as nourishing and warming as a cup of broth with a sprinkle of Parmesan on a cold winter day and there's hardly a better medicine than chicken broth when you're not feeling well. My friends can tell when I'm ailing. I put on a big pot of chicken broth.

After our tour of Paola's kitchen, we got together in my horse-stable apartment for predinner refreshments. Franco brought us wine and cheese, all with Paola's compliments. Besides the concrete horse trough, my apartment had huge wooden beams more than two hundred years old. It had a rustic stone floor and a giant-size fireplace. The apartment even had a tiny kitchen. My apartment's charm prepared us for a memorable dinner.

Dinner was at eight. The dining room, a converted horse stable, was full. Most of the guests had come from Castlefranco and the surrounding area. When we peeked into the dining room

Italian Pines   *Canonici*

on our arrival, it was cold and not very inviting. Now it was well heated by four large wood-burning stoves. Tables had linen cloths and autumn flowers. At each place there was a stack of several plates. In his journal, Bill says there were six plates. That's the Italian way; they don't like mixed flavors, so they change dishes for each course. I'd work in the kitchen or wait tables, but I wouldn't like to be an Italian dishwasher.

We had at least three types of *antipasto*, three pastas in addition to the tortellini, and for the main course, three roasted meats, two roasted vegetables and a salad. Desserts consisted of cream tart, fried cream and roasted chestnuts. Some dishes were seasoned with local balsamic vinegar. Modena, the world center for balsamic, is a ten-minute ride up the road. The after-dinner drink was made locally from walnut pits. I've been back to Villa Gaidello, but subsequent visits didn't have the same surprise as the first.

When you go to Villa Gaidello, be sure to go up the road to Modena. See the magnificent market in the center of town and taste balsamic vinegar in the local factories. Be sure to drive a few kilometers to Parma, where the best prosciutto is made, and to Reggio Emilia for Parmigiano Reggiano. The area is a gastronomic delight, an area skipped over by many American tourists.

Easy Pasta Sauces – No Cooking Required

When you visit *Nonna's* kitchen, you learn that there are countless ways for doing pasta. My relatives Ondina and Rosa take their portion of pasta directly from the colander before sauce is applied. Rosa puts a little Parmesan on hers. Ondina puts on a little raw olive oil and a sprinkling of Parmesan. Before the Second Vatican Council, when we had meatless Fridays, my mother would often serve pasta with a little oil, bread crumbs and parsley. Sometimes she added cooked green peas.

The basic tomato sauce (p.16) is used as a base for various pastas by adding one or two ingredients - canned tuna, green peas, fresh parsley, sautéed zucchini, diced eggplant and just about any other vegetable. Although there are many ways to do pasta, there's only one way to cook it. That's *al dente* in plenty of salted water.

Venice - vegetable market

Garlic, Olive Oil and Herbs

½ cup olive oil, sufficient to coat pasta

1 clove garlic (more if desired)

½ cup parsley

½ cup basil

Salt and freshly ground black pepper to taste

Optional: Other herbs according to preference

Finely chop the garlic, parsley and basil together. Mix with oil. Other herbs may be added. Season with salt and pepper to taste. Apply to hot pasta. Toss and serve.

Pasta with Basil and Bread Crumbs

½ cup chopped basil

1½ cups bread crumbs

Milk, sufficient to moisten bread crumbs

½ cup olive oil, sufficient to form dense sauce

Salt and freshly ground pepper, to taste

Optional: ½ medium onion, chopped

Moisten bread crumbs, squeeze out excess milk and mix with chopped basil. Stir in oil, salt and pepper. Pour on hot pasta and toss.

This sauce may be warmed over moderate heat, but do not cook. Warm oil in a pan and add basil mixture. Also, the onion may be sautéed over moderate heat. Then add basil mixture and stir. Spread over pasta. Toss and serve.

Pasta with Capers and Anchovy

½ cup capers

2 fillets of anchovies

1 clove garlic

½+ cup olive oil, sufficient to obtain a flowing sauce

Juice of 1 lemon

½ cup chopped parsley

Optional: pinch of red pepper flakes

If capers and anchovies are preserved under salt, wash them well. Grind capers, anchovies and garlic with mortar and pestle or in food processor. Gradually add oil to form a dense, flowing sauce. Add lemon juice and a half cup of chopped parsley and more oil if necessary to obtain desired density. Pour over hot pasta and toss. Before tossing, a pinch of red pepper flakes may be added.

Adriatic fishing camp

Butter and Parmesan Cheese

3 tablespoons butter

½ cup grated Parmesan cheese

Salt and freshly ground pepper to taste

Pour melted butter into a warm serving bowl. Add cooked pasta. Add Parmesan, salt and pepper. Toss and serve. While the butter is melting, you may wish to season it with four or five sage leaves.

Fresh Tomato Sauce

6 to 8 Roma tomatoes, seeded and excess liquid squeezed out

1 clove garlic, (amount may be reduced or garlic may be eliminated)

½ cup olive oil

¼ cup chopped basil

½ cup chopped parsley

Salt and freshly ground pepper to taste

Optional: Red pepper flakes and/or powder, Parmesan cheese, 1 tablespoon chopped fresh oregano may be substituted for basil and parsley.

Mix finely chopped tomatoes, garlic, basil and parsley. Add salt and pepper. Blend in olive oil to form a dense, flowing sauce. Pour sauce on hot pasta and toss.

Sprinkle with Parmesan cheese if desired.

Mozzarella, Tomato and Parmesan Cheese

4 Roma tomatoes, seeded and excess liquid squeezed out

8 tablespoons olive oil

1/3 pound mozzarella

2 tablespoons chopped basil

1 tablespoon chopped fresh oregano

Salt and freshly ground pepper to taste

4 tablespoons grated Parmesan cheese

Optional: capers, chopped green or black olives

Slice tomatoes into thin strips and mix in a bowl with the basil, oregano and Parmesan. Cover and refrigerate for at least 3 hours. While the pasta is cooking, dice mozzarella and spread over bottom of serving bowl. Put drained pasta over mozzarella and toss rapidly. Pour on tomato mixture, salt and pepper, and toss again. Serve immediately.

Basic Pesto

During basil season I make a basic pesto consisting of basil leaves, oil and salt. I freeze the basic pesto in ice trays and store the cubes in plastic bags. When I need pesto during the year, I thaw the amount of pesto I need and add fresh ingredients. The basic pesto can also be used to season soups and sauces when fresh basil is not available.

8 or 10 cups fresh basil leaves

1 cup olive oil

Sea salt to taste

Blend the ingredients in blender or food chopper and freeze. When you are ready to use the pesto, thaw desired quantity of frozen pesto and add:

1 garlic clove, finely chopped, per pound of pasta

1 or 2 tablespoons olive oil, sufficient to coat pasta

1 or 2 tablespoons melted butter

Parmesan cheese, freshly grated

Optional: 1 teaspoon marjoram, 1/4 cup toasted pine nuts

Cook pasta *al dente* and toss with just enough pesto to coat the pasta. Use plenty of cheese.

Enhanced Pesto

1 1/2 to 2 cups basil leaves

1 cup parsley

1 clove garlic

1/2+ cup olive oil

3 Roma tomatoes, seeded, excess liquid squeezed out and chopped

1/4 pound mozzarella, diced

Salt and pepper/red pepper flakes to taste

With mortar and pestle or in food processor, grind basil, parsley and garlic. Gradually add olive oil, salt, freshly ground pepper/red pepper flakes. When a dense fluid sauce has formed, add chopped tomatoes and diced mozzarella. Do not grind tomatoes and mozzarella. Put hot pasta in a pan over moderate heat, pour on sauce, toss briefly over heat and serve.

The Best Tortellini

It was by pure chance that I discovered a restaurant with the best tortellini I've ever had. A friend and I were driving north on Autostrada A-1 from Florence to Bologna. Our intention was to bypass Bologna, but Bologna is known for tortellini. Looking to satisfy our craving for tortellini, we decided to exit just before Bologna at Rioveggio. You won't find the place on most maps.

At the exit station we asked if there was a restaurant nearby. We were directed to La Fornace, so named because there was once a brick furnace at that location. A kilometer or two straight ahead we found La Fornace, a restaurant and small hotel.

The large dining room was almost full of people who seemed to be local workers, a good sign. Local Italians know where to find good food. The waitress directed us to a table near a window that looked out on a yard with peacocks, chickens and interesting looking ducks. Determined to get our fill of tortellini, we ordered two types, *tortellini in brodo* (in broth) and tortellini with a Bolognese sauce (p.19). We asked for "a little" prosciutto to munch on while we waited for the tor-

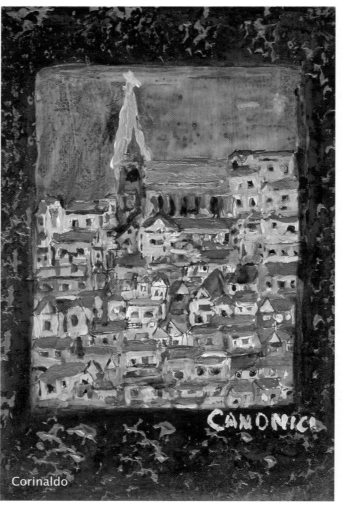

Corinaldo

tellini. I don't think our waitress understood the word "*poco*" (little). She brought a huge plate of beautiful prosciutto made locally. Then came the *tortellini in brodo*. They were the tiniest tortellini I had ever seen, handmade in the restaurant. Finally, we got the tortellini with Bolognese sauce. Both were good beyond description. I've returned to La Fornace several times and have always found the place delightful. One visit was during the Christmas holidays and there was snow on the ground. The peacocks and ducks were on the side porch protected from the cold. I've missed the birds on recent visits. They're no longer around. I suppose the owner decided they should go because of the bird flu scare.

Good service greatly enhances a meal, and good service depends on the person waiting tables. The only waitress at La Fornace is Amabile. The name means "loveable". Amabile has a loveable, welcoming disposition. She moves about the restaurant like a butterfly and keeps everybody happy. I hope someday you will stop by La Fornace to meet Amabile and to check out her prosciutto and homemade tortellini.

Tortellini

Various combinations of meats are used for tortellini filling depending on region and personal taste. In Bologna, known for its tortellini, the filling usually consists of turkey breast (or capon), pork, prosciutto and Parmesan.

3 tablespoons butter

¼ **pound pork loin**

¼ **pound turkey breast**

¼ **pound mortadella**

¼ **pound prosciutto**

1 bay leaf

½ **to** ¾ **cup grated Parmesan**

Pinch of nutmeg

1 egg

Salt and pepper

Cut pork and turkey into small pieces and cook in butter with bay leaf. Remove bay leaf and allow meats to cool.

In a food processor combine the pork, turkey, drippings from cooking pan, mortadella and prosciutto. Grind, but do not puree. Mix meats with cheese, nutmeg, egg, salt and pepper. Cover and refrigerate for 4 hours or overnight.

The dough for tortellini is treated like the dough used for ravioli (p.42), but always cut in rounds, 1¾ to 2 inches.

Place a teaspoon of filling on each round. Moisten the edges of the round with egg or water. Fold the round, forming a crescent, enclosing the filling. Seal the edges by pressing with your fingers or the prongs of a fork. Then bring the two ends of the crescent together, overlapping them and twisting one end over the other. Seal the ends. The sealed edges should be curved up, in the shape of a little hat. Tortellini are sometimes called *cappelletti*, little hats.

Spread the finished tortellini on a cloth. Turn after about 30 minutes so the tortellini can dry on both sides.

The Marche - Cousin Magiorino's house

Ravioli

For the dough:

- 3 cups flour
- 4 eggs
- Salt to taste
- 2 tablespoons water

Select a filling:

Ricotta filling:

- 2½ cups ricotta, well drained
- 2 eggs
- ½ to 1 cup grated Parmesan
- Salt and pepper to taste

Cheese and spinach (or Swiss chard) filling:

- 2½ cups ricotta or Pecorino
- 2½ cups spinach or Swiss chard, cooked and very finely chopped
- 2 eggs
- Pinch of nutmeg
- Salt and pepper to taste

Italian-American versions of filling:
Corinne Borgognoni Rocconi (Lake Village, AR):

- 2 pounds lean beef, ground
- 1 pound lean pork, ground
- 1½ pounds chicken, ground
- ½ pound turkey, ground
- 1 can (16 ounces) tomatoes, drained and chopped
- 1 cup grated Parmesan
- 6 eggs
- ½ pound cracker crumbs
- 8 dark green lettuce leaves, chopped

Gigia Sampaolesi Pieroni and Theresa Reginelli Pieroni (Lake Village, AR):

- 2 sirloin steaks, ground
- 2 chickens, boned, ground
- 4 pork chops, ground
- 1 can pork brains, chopped
- 1 can mushrooms, finely chopped
- 2 or 3 ribs celery, finely chopped
- 1 small onion, finely chopped
- 1 clove garlic, finely chopped
- 1 package crackers, crumbled and moistened
- 7 to 8 eggs
- 1 cup Romano cheese

Making the dough:

Put the flour in a bowl or on a countertop. Make a well in the flour. Break eggs into the well and add salt. Beat the eggs with a fork and gradually pull in and mix flour and egg with your hands.

Work the dough, adding a few drops of water if the dough is too dry. If the dough is too moist, add a little flour. Knead the dough in a rolling motion, pushing it away from you with the heels of your hands. Knead until the dough is smooth. The dough should remain somewhat soft but not sticky. When the kneading is complete, break the dough into 6 or 8 pieces, roll into balls, then flatten the balls somewhat, and oil them slightly to prevent drying. Put the balls in separate plastic bags. Wrap the dough in a cloth and allow it to rest for 1 hour. In the meantime, prepare filling for the ravioli.

Making the filling:

In Italy ravioli are filled with either cheese alone or cheese and spinach or Swiss chard. Some Italian-Americans use meat fillings for ravioli, similar to the filling that Italians use for tortellini.

All meats and vegetables used in ravioli filling are cooked and finely chopped. Then all ingredients are well mixed.

Roll the dough either by hand or machine. Roll a piece of dough at a time to keep the dough from drying. Cut the dough into pieces about 2 to 2½ inches, either squares or circles. Put a teaspoon of filling in the center of half of the pieces of dough. Moisten the outer edge of the dough with either beaten egg or water, and cover with another piece of dough. Seal the edges by pressing with your fingers or with the prongs of a fork.

Allow the filled ravioli to rest on a floured surface for 30 minutes to 1 hour. Then cook in plenty of salted water.

Ravioli may be served with a tomato sauce or with melted butter. If you use a butter sauce, try seasoning the butter with a few leaves of sage. Whatever sauce is used, sprinkle generously with Parmesan or Pecorino.

Venice - Ponte della Guerra

Abruzzo - Scanno

An Out of the Way Place

It was the end of May and the beginning of June, 2006. After having accompanied a friend around The Marche Region of Italy, I had a few unplanned days all to myself. So I decided to search out a remote village where I might spend some time in a rustic environment. One of my relatives suggested Scanno, a mountain village in the region of Abruzzo, made famous by the well-known photographer from Senigallia, Mario Giacomelli. All I knew about Scanno was what Giacomelli portrayed in his photographs: old women dressed in traditional long black dresses and headdress. I decided to go to Scanno, hoping to experience a people and lifestyle of the late eighteen-hundreds.

I took a train to Pescara and there changed to another train to Sulmona, 73 kilometers inland. The train from Pescara was crowded with high school students who displayed all the vitality and loudness typical of older adolescents. The school day was over and they were returning to their homes. A few got off at every stop as the train moved inland toward Sulmona.

Sulmona is the largest town in the area and serves as a center of commerce for other villages on the outskirts of the Apennine Mountains. It is known for the production of *confetti*, candy-coated almonds used to celebrate baptisms, confirmations, weddings and other festive occasions. I had to take a bus for the next 31 kilometers to Scanno.

Scanno looks like a Swiss mountain village. Even the cool evening air is reminiscent of the Alps. I got off the bus in the town square and, with backpack over my right shoulder, wandered around the town hoping to find lodging in a home where I could have home-cooked meals with a family. I stopped to chat with two ladies, Anna and Celestina, who were taking their afternoon stroll (*passeggiata*). They told me that Scanno did not have the kind of place I was looking for, but recommended the Hotel Belvedere in the center of town next to the church. It was an excellent choice.

At the hotel desk, I met Francesco, the owner. They call him Chiccio. He's an elderly man who walks with a cane. I also met Filomena, one of the ladies who still wears the traditional long black dress and headpiece. She told me she had worked at the hotel sixty years. Chiccio assigned me a room with a beautiful mountain view.

That evening, beginning at 9:30, there was Mass in the church next door to the hotel and a procession through the town. It was the last day of May and the procession was in honor of Mary. Two young men carried a small statue of Mary attached to a wooden frame that rested on their shoulders. The different church organizations wore their groups' distinctive colors. Leading the procession, in front of the statue, there were ten or twelve robed acolytes carrying candles. There were lighted candles on balconies and in windows along the procession's route up and down steep steps through the village. Bells rang out from the town's several belfries. Old people who could not walk in the procession stood on balconies and in doorways. They lined the streets reciting the rosary and singing along with those in the procession. When the statue passed by they made the Sign of the Cross. I was moved by their expression of faith.

The next afternoon, beginning at 4 o'clock, I took part in another procession. Now that May was over, the little statue of the Madonna was returned to its usual resting place in a little chapel down on the side of Lake Scanno, about five kilometers from the center of town. A lady on the bus back to Sulmona related to me the history behind the little statue. Four or five hundred years ago a shepherd saw a light on the mountainside near the lake. After observing the light on several successive nights, he went to tell the parish priest what he had seen, and together they went to investigate the mysterious light. On the side of the mountain overlooking Lake Scanno, they found a wooden statue of the Madonna about two feet tall. They left the statue in its place and proceeded to build a chapel around it. Twenty-five years ago the statue was stolen and never found, so community leaders commissioned a sculptor to make a replica to take its place. Today a paved road runs beside the lake under a portion of the chapel.

The dialect of the people is indicative of Scanno's remoteness. I could not understand them when they talked among themselves. Though remote, Scanno is not the rustic village I had expected. There are a number of hotels and restaurants, some open only in winter and mid-summer to accommodate visitors who come for winter sports and to avoid the summer heat.

I inquired whether there was a restaurant that served food typical of the area and was referred to Ristorante Costanza e Roberto. Costanza suggested I try her *pasta alla chitarra* with tomato sauce. I ordered a mixed *antipasto* of cheeses and *salumi* and the *chittara*. Costanza also brought a sampling of *gnocchetti* with broccoli and chickpeas.

I later found that the *gnocchetti* (p.52), made with flour alone, is one of the two most typical dishes of the area. The other is polenta with beans.

I want to go back to Scanno, and I want to explore the mountainside beyond the resort area. There I will find that rustic place that has no hotels or restaurants, where I can live with Italian mountain people and eat their food.

On the heels of Jesi

Lasagna

In the Region of The Marche, and nowhere else, lasagna is called *Vincisgrassi*. Some say the name "*Vincisgrassi*" is derived from Windish Graetz, Napoleon's general who occupied Ancona in 1799. According to this theory, the Austrian general's personal chef invented the pasta dish that became Windish Graetz's favorite. Others claim that the pasta dish was already in existence before the Napoleonic Wars of 1799. In a publication of 1780, Antonio Nebbia, a chef from Macerata, Marche Region, describes a sauce for "*Princisgras*". This latter theory claims that in time the name "*Princisgras*" became "*Vincisgrassi*."

Vincisgrassi

The basic ingredients of lasagna consist of sheets of pasta dough, a béchamel sauce and a meatsauce. Older recipes for the meatsauce contained the outer extremities and the inner organs of chickens (*rigalie di pollo*) and the brain and sweetbreads of calves (*cervella, filoni e animelle*).

Sheets of dough, sufficient to make 5 or 6 layers in a baking pan approximately 8 x 10 inches

For the meatsauce:

1 pound ground beef

Olive oil

1 onion, chopped

2 ribs celery, chopped

1 carrot, chopped

1 can (28 ounces) tomato puree (*passato*) or diced tomatoes

Salt and pepper to taste

Brown the beef in olive oil. Add onion, celery and carrot and cook about 10 minutes. Add tomatoes, salt and pepper. Cook for an additional hour. The sauce should have a thick, fluid consistency. If it appears to get too dry, add a little water. If it is too fluid, cook a little longer.

For béchamel sauce:

6 tablespoons butter

6 tablespoons flour

1 quart milk

Zest of 1 lemon

Salt

Melt butter in saucepan. Add flour and whisk until blended.

In another saucepan, bring milk to a boil. Add milk and lemon zest to flour, stirring rapidly to blend. Cook over low heat for 15 minutes or until sauce thickens.

Cut the dough into manageable sheets, about 4 x 6 inches. Cook sheets in salted water, a few at a time, about 2 minutes for fresh pasta. Remove sheets, one at a time, and spread on clean damp cloth.

Cover bottom of buttered baking pan with liquid from meatsauce. Then cover the bottom with 1 layer of cooked lasagna sheets. Cover the layer lightly with meatsauce. Then spread on béchamel sauce lightly. Finally sprinkle generously with Parmesan. Repeat the layering process for 5 or 6 layers if the baking pan permits. Be sure to allow sufficient space for sauce to bubble without spilling over.

Dot the top layer with butter, after sauces and Parmesan. Cook in preheated oven at 400° for 25 minutes. Allow lasagna to rest 15 minutes before serving.

Senigallia - a view from Via Verde

Cheese Lasagna (Lasagnette alla Bava)

1 pound lasagna strips

½ pound fontina cheese

8 tablespoons (1 stick) butter

Salt

Grated Parmesan cheese

Cook lasagna dough *al dente* in boiling salted water. Drain well and butter the strips well with half the butter. In a buttered baking dish, layer the lasagna strips alternately with slices of fontina, beginning with the lasagna strips. Top with melted butter and Parmesan. Bake in a preheated 400º oven for 10 minutes.

Region: Valle d'Aosta

Gnocchi

Classic Gnocchi

1 pound baking potatoes

Vegetable oil

Salt and pepper

1 egg

½ cup, plus 2 tablespoons all-purpose flour, divided

Preheat oven to 400º.

Season potatoes with vegetable oil, salt and pepper. Place on a baking sheet and bake until tender, about 1 to 1½ hours. Potatoes may be boiled but care must be taken to prevent the potatoes from absorbing too much water. Do not cut the potatoes before boiling. If potatoes are to be boiled, do not season with the oil, salt and pepper before cooking, but do salt the cooking water.

Whether potatoes are baked or boiled, allow them to cool. Peel and mash the potatoes, with a hand potato masher, until smooth. Season with salt and pepper. Add the egg and ¼ cup plus 2 tablespoons flour and mix to form a dough. Sprinkle the remaining ¼ cup flour on a kneading board or clean countertop. Turn the dough onto the floured surface and roll into a log, about 1-inch thick. Cut the dough into 1-inch pieces. Roll each piece across the tines of a fork. My mother used to press the gnocchi with her index finger, giving a backward spin.

Cook the gnocchi in plenty boiling salted water for about 5 minutes; the gnocchi should float to the top when cooked. Remove the gnocchi with a slotted spoon and drain.

A popular sauce for gnocchi is a tomato duck sauce. However, other tomato or cream sauces also work well with gnocchi.

Gnocchi in Broth

1 pound white potatoes, boiled whole with skin

¼ pound ground beef

¼ pound calf liver, finely chopped

2 eggs

2 medium onions, chopped

Chopped parsley

Pinch of marjoram

Pinch of nutmeg

Salt and pepper

Butter

Beef broth

Parmesan cheese

Peel boiled potatoes and mash well. Add ground beef, liver, marjoram, nutmeg, salt and pepper. Mix well. Add egg and mix again. From the mixture, form gnocchi the shape and size of ping-pong balls.

Fry onion in butter until lightly golden. Add gnocchi and fry, at first over low heat, and then over high heat until brown on all sides.

Put 4 or 5 gnocchi in each person's bowl. Top with a spoon full of onion and cover with hot beef broth. Sprinkle with Parmesan and serve immediately.

This can be a nutritious, one-dish meal.

Region: Friuli Venezia Giulia

Ricotta Gnocchi

3 cups ricotta

2½ cups flour

½ cup bread crumbs

Salt

Butter

Grated Parmesan

Work the ricotta with a whisk until it becomes smooth and creamy. Add the flour, bread crumbs, salt and a little water, just enough to bring the ingredients together as a dough. If the dough is sticky, add a little more flour.

Roll the dough into little logs about ¾-inch thick. Cut into 1-inch-long pieces. Boil gently in salted water for about 7 minutes. Gnocchi should float to the top when cooked. Remove gnocchi with a slotted spoon and drain well. Season with melted butter and Parmesan. If hazelnuts are available, sprinkle also with chopped hazelnuts. Serve hot.

Region: Trentino Alto Adige

Bread Gnocchi

During hard times Italians used only those garden and animal products that were available in their homes and immediate surroundings. They wasted nothing. Old bread was recycled in the form of bread crumbs, croutons, pulp for soups and as the base ingredient for various dishes. In the Alpine Region of Friuli Venezia Giulia, they made gnocchi from old bread moistened with milk.

8 cups old bread, cut into small pieces

Milk, for moistening bread

1 cup finely chopped ham

1 cup finely chopped prosciutto

1 cup finely chopped *pancetta* or lean bacon

2 eggs

3 tablespoons flour

2 tablespoons chopped chives or green onions

1 cup grated Parmesan

Salt and pepper

Butter, melted

Put bread in a bowl and cover with milk. Allow bread and milk to rest about 1 hour, until the milk is absorbed. Squeeze milk from bread until bread is just moist. Add ham, prosciutto, *pancetta*/bacon, flour, eggs, Parmesan, salt and pepper. Mix well.

Form mixture into gnocchi the shape and size of ping-pong balls. Allow gnocchi to rest for 1 hour.

Gently boil gnocchi in salted water for ½ hour. Drain well and put in individual serving bowls. Sprinkle gnocchi with Parmesan and chopped chives. Pour on melted butter and serve.

Bread gnocchi are also good with a tomato sauce or a Bolognese sauce.

Region: Friuli Venezia Giulia

Chicken Gnocchi / *Gnocchi di Pollo*

2 cups boiled chicken, finely chopped

2 cups mashed potatoes, cooked as for regular gnocchi (p.48)

2 eggs, plus 1 egg yolk

2 tablespoons lemon zest

Pinch of nutmeg

Salt and pepper

Mix all ingredients. Form mixture into gnocchi the shape and size of ping-pong balls and roll them in flour. Bring plenty salted water to a boil. Add a few gnocchi at a time and cook, gently, about 5 to 10 minutes.

Serve with butter and Parmesan cheese.

The chicken gnocchi may be cooked and served in broth. Bring broth to a boil. Add gnocchi and cook gently for 5 minutes. Add the juice of ½ lemon. Cook an additional 5 minutes. Serve in a bowl with broth, Parmesan on the side.

Assisi - S. Pietro

An Assisi Street

Gnocchetti Made with Flour Alone

2 cups flour

Salt to taste

1 cup warm water, divided

Place flour in a bowl. Make a small well in the flour. Add salt and ½ cup warm water. Mix well. Then add more water to form a soft dough.

Place dough on a floured board and work in more flour to form a soft dough. Form the dough into a ball, wrap it with a clean cloth and allow to rest for 1 hour.

Form rolls the size of a little finger and cut the dough into 1 to 1 ½ inch pieces. With finger, press each piece, rolling backward, to form an indentation. Allow *gnocchetti* to rest on a floured surface.

Cook in plenty salted water. Remove from water with slotted spoon. Dress with sauce of preference and Parmesan cheese.

Gnocchetti may be served with heavy cream alone or with butter alone and Parmesan.

St. Francis - a collage

Assisi - Basilica of St. Francis

Assisi - from B&B Window - 11-14-03 (angelica)

My Favorite Place

My favorite place in the whole world is Assisi, home of St. Francis. I usually begin my visits to Assisi with a stop at Santa Maria degli Angeli, near the train station, in the valley below the town of Assisi. The grand Basilica of Santa Maria degli Angeli (St. Mary of the Angels) was built in the fifteen hundreds. Inside the massive structure is the Portiuncula, the tiny church that St. Francis restored. There you can also see the hermitage where St. Francis died.

On my first visit to Assisi in 1972, I arrived by train, stored my luggage at the station and walked the road up to Assisi, about six kilometers. The fields were gold with wheat ready for harvest, and Assisi, the magnificent medieval jewel, sat enthroned on the mountain ahead of me. I took pictures all the way, trying to capture the moment and hold it forever.

I had planned to make just a brief visit to Assisi, then return to the train station for my luggage and move on. In Assisi a summer afternoon rain had cooled the town and birds circled above. I had the feeling that the birds and St. Francis were beckoning me to stay for a while. So I took a taxi to the train station, got my luggage and returned to Assisi for the night. I was completely enthralled by the town, its narrow ascending and descending alleys, window boxes of bright red geraniums, colorful flags brightening the elegant medieval stone structures and narrow cobblestone streets. The spirit of St. Francis was surely there.

What moves me most about Assisi is to stand beside and touch the tomb of St. Francis in the crypt of the awesome Basilica. People from every country and every religious belief come by the thousands day after day to venerate the *poveretto*, the humble saint. The reverence of their demeanor shows that they come to Assisi, not as tourists, but as pilgrims.

A special spiritual experience is to visit Francis' favorite hermitage, *Eremo delle Carcere*, an hour's walk up Mt. Subasio. If you cannot walk to the hermitage, you can get there by car. Try to get to the hermitage in early morning, when you can walk the trail alone, hear the chirping birds and see the tiny crosses placed in the crevices of stones by someone who was there before you. The coolness of the morning air, the ancient twisted trees protruding from rocks and the subtle sounds mixed with sacred silence will recharge your soul.

There are many good eating places down in the valley from Assisi, toward Santa Maria degli Angeli. There are good restaurants in Assisi as well, but those in Assisi are generally more expensive than those in the valley. I know two restaurants in the town of Assisi that are good and reasonably priced. Al Camino Vecchio is around the corner and up the hill from Beata Angelina, the convent where I stay when I'm in Assisi.

For atmosphere and reasonably priced good food, I like I Monici on the main street, Via Scalette, uphill toward the center of Assisi. I Monici is a quaint restaurant I discovered on a trip with Pam and Kerry Minninger. Agnello, the owner and chef, prepares what you want, even if it's not on the menu. Annalisa, his daughter, is head waitress and does her best to please guests. Their tagliatelle with Bolognese sauce (p.19) will give you a good reason to go back to the restaurant.

Near Assisi is the town of Deruta, known worldwide for high quality ceramics called "*majolica*". Deruta potters get their good clay from the banks of the Tiber that flows by the town on its way to Rome and beyond. After you have finished your shopping at Cama, Miriam or any of Deruta's many ceramic shops, you may enjoy lunch at La Fontanella near the center of town. On a recent visit to Deruta, Steve Frattini and I had a great lunch there, only grilled vegetables (p.128) from La Fontanella's buffet. Notice their colorful dishes and tabletops. Deruta specializes in functional pottery.

Temple of minerva

Primi 55

Risotto

Basic Risotto

Following the steps for making Basic Risotto, Italian cooks create their own types and flavors of risotto according to vegetables, meats or fish they have on hand.

6+ cups meat stock (p.64)

¼ cup olive oil

½ cup finely chopped yellow onion

2 cups rice - The best rice for risotto is one that releases the most starch and absorbs the most liquid and flavors. Italians prefer Arborio, Carnaroli or Vialone Nano.

1 cup dry white wine - Use a good quality wine, one you would drink.

2 tablespoons unsalted butter

½ cup grated Parmesan and additional Parmesan to be served on the side

Salt, if needed

Before starting the risotto, bring the stock to a gentle boil and maintain a simmer during the cooking process. Start by heating olive oil in a wide pan with a heavy bottom and cook onion until it is transparent. The onion used in risotto is usually yellow. Shallots, leeks or green onions may be used according to flavor desired. If garlic is used, it is added during this first phase of cooking.

When the onion has softened, about 3 or 4 minutes, add unwashed rice and stir with a wooden spoon until all grains are well coated with oil and translucent with a little white dot in the center, about 3 or 4 minutes. Add wine and deglaze pan by scraping the bottom and sides of the pan with the wooden spoon. Allow the wine to completely evaporate.

Add boiling stock a ladle at a time, stirring constantly in broad strokes extending to the bottom and sides of the pan. Wait until the stock is absorbed before adding the next ladle, but keep the rice well moist and somewhat fluid. When the rice is tender *al dente* and creamy, about 20 minutes. Additional ingredients, precooked or quick cooking, may be added. Allow everything to warm through. Remove the risotto from heat and stir in unsalted butter. If cheese is required, stir it in at this time. The process should work with most kinds of risotto.

Risotto Milanese

The distinctive ingredient of Risotto Milanese is saffron. It is served with *Ossobuco* (p.83).

6+ cups meat stock (p.64)

2 tablespoons pancetta, prosciutto or lean bacon

¼ cup olive oil

½ cup finely chopped yellow onion

1 cup dry white wine

2 cups Arborio rice (Carnaroli or Vialone Nano)

⅓ teaspoon powdered saffron or, ½ teaspoon chopped saffron strands, dissolved in 1 cup hot stock

2 tablespoons unsalted butter

⅓+ cup Parmesan cheese

Salt and pepper

Bring stock to a slow simmer and dissolve saffron in 1 cup of stock. Heat oil, add meat and onion. Cook until onion is transparent.

Add rice and stir until grains are coated with oil and translucent with a little white dot in the center. Then add wine and allow it to evaporate.

Add stock a ladle at a time, stirring constantly. Wait until stock is almost completely absorbed before adding the next ladleful. For the fourth addition, use the cup of stock with saffron.

When the rice is cooked *al dente* and creamy, about 20 minutes, remove from heat. Stir in butter, cheese and half a ladle of stock. Add salt and pepper to taste. Stir and serve with grated Parmesan on the side.

Risotto with Clams or Lump Crab

6 cups beef stock, fish stock or water

1 to 2 cups baby clams with juices, or 1 to 2 cups lump crabmeat

¼ cup olive oil

½ cup finely chopped yellow onion

2 cups rice (Arborio, Carnaroli or Vialone Nano)

1 cup dry white wine

2 tablespoons unsalted butter

Salt and pepper to taste

Bring stock or water to a slow boil and maintain simmer. Some Italians prefer water for a fish risotto.

Heat oil, add onion and cook until transparent. Add rice and stir until all grains are well coated with oil and translucent, with a little white dot in the center. Add wine and allow it to evaporate.

Add stock/water a ladle at a time, stirring constantly. Wait until stock is almost completely absorbed before adding the next ladleful.

When rice is cooked *al dente* and creamy, about 20 minutes, stir in clams/crabmeat, cook 1 or 2 minutes. Remove from heat. Stir in butter. Add salt and pepper. Stir and serve.

Florence - Duomo and rooftops

Primi 57

The Charm of Polenta

Polenta is one of those Italian dishes that has gone from rustic to chic. At the end of the 1800s and early 1900s, when times were hard and Italians were coming to America by the thousands, polenta was served daily in many Italian houses. In some parts of central and northern Italy, it was the principal winter food. Many families in those areas had polenta for both lunch and dinner, and sometimes leftovers were grilled or fried for breakfast.

In our home we made polenta in a soft consistency and served it on a board that covered most of the table. That was the way Italians from The Marche Region of Italy made it. A simple sauce was spread over the top, and if there was a little meat or sausage, pieces were spread out over the polenta. The rule of the game in our home was that you had to eat your way to the piece of meat or sausage. You could not just reach out and get the meat. In regions toward the north of Italy, polenta had a thicker consistency. It was also served on a board forming somewhat of a mound in the center. A small furrow, along the center of the polenta held the sauce and kept it from running over the board. Since polenta with a thicker consistency lay toward the center of the board, each family member scooped a portion to his place with his fork or spoon. If there was meat or fish,

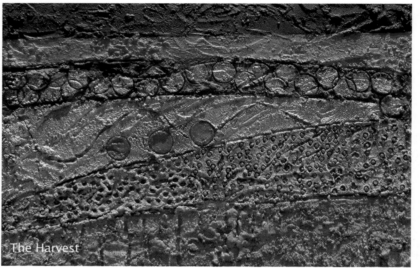

The Harvest

a piece was put at each person's place. My 95-year-old cousin, Vanda, remembers when pasta was also spread down the center of the board. Families were large, extended families, and more often than not there wasn't sufficient space at the table for everyone to be seated. Men and children sat while women ate standing behind children.

The copper pot used to make the polenta was called the *paiolo*. It hung in the center of the fireplace and there was a stool or bench close by for the person who stirred the polenta. The cooking process requires constant stirring for 40 to 45 minutes. The ingredients are simple, just water, cornmeal and a little salt. Italians use yellow cornmeal for polenta, but I have found that white meal works equally well. In the mountainous northern regions of Italy where dairy products are plentiful, milk was sometimes used as the liquid ingredient for polenta.

Polenta is best when served on a board or wooden plate, especially polenta with a fluid consistency, because wood absorbs some of the liquid and prevents flowing, making the polenta more manageable for eating.

During hard times, Italians seasoned polenta with pieces of salt meat fried in homemade lard or with a sauce made with little birds. In our home a favorite was wild rabbit in a tomato sauce. Today polenta is a restaurant delicacy, usually served baked or grilled. Our grandparents and great-grandparents would be amused to find that their peasant food has been elevated to such elegant status.

Use the sauce of your choice on polenta. Meat sauces and sauces with pieces of sausage are especially good. Most sauces are complimented by Parmesan or Pecorino cheese. Italians generally do not use cheese with a fish sauce.

The polenta that I call basic is the polenta that we had in our home, the thinner consistency that is spread about a half-inch thick on a board or plate and covered with sauce. My brother, Joe, uses 5 cups of water to 1 cup of cornmeal, but you may find this too thin for your taste. Joe also recommends that you let the polenta sit about five minutes to form a slight film before applying the sauce.

For polenta in a truly Marchigiana[1] style, make a sauce with about a cup of diced pancetta and a half pound of sausage freed of casing, cut into bite-size pieces and sautéed with a finely chopped onion. Spread the sauce over polenta on a board while it is still hot. I use individual wooden plates.

[1]Marchigiana refers to the Region of the Marche, on the Adriatic Coast of Central Italy

Countryside of S. Angelo

CANONIC

Basic Polenta

5 cups water

2 teaspoons salt or to taste

1 cup cornmeal, preferably yellow but white will work

Bring 4 cups water to a boil. Dissolve cornmeal in 1 cup cold water.

Remove boiling water from heat and gradually pour in dissolved cornmeal, stirring constantly with a long-handled wooden spoon.

Put pot on medium to low heat and stir constantly for 40 minutes or until cooked. Heat should be just high enough to cause a very gentle boil. My brother says he can tell by smell when the polenta is cooked. I can't. The cooked polenta will tend to pull away from the side of the pot. If the polenta tends to harden too quickly before it is cooked, add a little hot water. For polenta with a thick consistency use 4 cups water to 1 cup cornmeal.

If you intend to grill, bake or fry the polenta, you must make it several hours in advance. Polenta can be refrigerated for several days, but it must be sealed well in foil or plastic wrap.

Polenta with Pumpkin

½ cup yellow cornmeal

½ cup white cornmeal

1 cup pumpkin or butternut squash, boiled and pureed

5 cups water

Salt to taste, about 2 teaspoons

4 tablespoons butter

Bring 4 cups water to a boil and add salt.

In the meantime, mix the two cornmeals and dissolve well in 1 cup cold water. Remove boiling water from heat and stir in dissolved cornmeal. Return pot to heat and maintain a very gentle boil, stirring constantly with a long-handled wooden spoon, always in the same direction, scraping mixture from bottom and sides of the pot. Polenta should cook in 40 minutes.

Before removing polenta from heat, stir in butter and pumpkin/squash puree. Spread polenta about 1/2-inch-thick on board or plate, or put it in a bowl.

Polenta may be eaten hot or cold, with or without sauce. Alpine Italians like it hot with a cold glass of milk or cold with hot milk. Leftovers may be fried or grilled. Slice polenta with a string or wire.

Region: Friuli Venezia Giulia

Arcevia

Baked Polenta with Sausage and Tomato Sauce

Baked polentas are all prepared more or less the same way. The difference is the sauce used between layers of polenta. Since the polenta is to be layered, one might want to double or triple the recipe prescribed for basic polenta. If a larger quantity of polenta is used, it will be more manageable if it is poured into a large bowl and allowed to cool. Wet the inside of the bowl before the polenta is poured. When you are ready to slice it, turn the bowl upside down and the polenta should come right out. Slice it about ¼-inch-thick with a strong string or fine wire.

In the Province of Molise a sausage and tomato sauce is put between layers. Begin by heating olive oil in a skillet. Then add skinned sausage and cook until the sausage is browned. Crumble the sausage and add basic tomato sauce (p.16). Season with salt and red pepper flakes.

Butter a baking dish and make alternate layers of polenta and sauce. Sprinkle each layer with Parmesan and Pecorino cheese and dot with butter. Top with butter and cheese. Bake for 1 hour at 375º. The polenta should have a golden crust. To serve, cut through the layers with a spatula and serve in slices.

Region: Molise

Spinach Polenta

1 cup cooked spinach (fresh or frozen)

1 cup yellow cornmeal

1 tablespoon all-purpose flour

1 stick (8 tablespoons) butter

2 cloves garlic

Salt and pepper

Cook spinach. Reserve cooking water. Chop finely.

In a 4 or 5 quart saucepan sauté garlic in butter until light golden. Add flour and cook, constantly stirring, until flour turns golden. Add spinach, salt and pepper. Cook about 10 minutes.

Gradually add water used to cook spinach plus additional water to total 5 cups of liquid. Allow to boil for 15 minutes. Gradually add cornmeal, stirring constantly to avoid lumping. Cook for 20 to 25 minutes.

This is a typical meal for poor mountain folks on a cold winter day.

Region: Friuli Venezia Giulia

The storm

CANONICI

When in Tuscany

When I go to Florence, I like to take in some other Tuscan towns. Siena is a must, and on my way to Siena I like to drive a few kilometers out of the way to San Gimignano, a beautifully restored, medieval town with fourteen towers. In medieval times there were more than seventy towers. My first visit to San Gimignano was in the nineteen-seventies with my niece Elizabeth. I think I liked it better then. It was in its first phase of restoration and much less touristy. The town has beautiful shops and a great selection of meats, cheeses and wines. If I am traveling with two or three friends, I like to get a supply of food and beverages for a picnic spread at Monteregione, a medieval walled compound on the way to Siena. Monteregione is hardly larger than a city block, but well worth an hour's stop.

The people of Siena boast about their city's clean-cut youth and say that Siena has not sold out to tourism. Words cannot describe Siena's eloquent charm and peacefulness. There's no wonder the city has given the world such great saints as St. Catherine.

My friend Elaine Trigiani lives in Loro Ciuffenna, a Tuscan village about 40 minutes southeast of Florence. She went there because, while researching her mother's Sicilian ancestry, she became interested in the olive oil business. Elaine spent 7 years learning about olive oil and Tuscan culinary traditions from lo-

PALAZZO Vecchio
Firenze

San Gimignano

cal producers, farmers, home cooks and chefs. She now conducts olive oil tasting seminars and olive oil cooking classes in Italy and in the United States. Her culinary programs include visits to Tuscan markets, wineries and olive oil mills. Certified as an olive oil taster by the Region of Tuscany, Elaine creates recipes using olive oil. She shared with me an old Loro Ciuffenna cookie recipe using all olive oil, the way the cookie was originally made (p.147).

When I visited Lora Ciuffenna with Elaine's mother, Jean Canizaro Enochs, and two other friends, Elaine took us to Gorgiti, an ancient mountain village where Grazia, the baker, gave us hot bread from her wood-fired oven and Anibale Baldi showed us his chestnut mill that operates from a mountain stream and runs constantly day and night. No one knows how long the mill has been in operation. Three men clad in heavy wool trousers came out to talk with us. They told us the village was founded by deserters from Hannibal's (Anibale) army. During wartime it served as a hiding place for people from Loro Ciuffenna and other towns in the valley. The haven, accessible only by a narrow rough road that barely accommodates a single car, has the appearance of a good hideout. Italy still has enchanting out-of-the-way places off the beaten path of tourists, but you have to search them out unless you have a guide like Elaine.

Broths, Minestras and Soups

Minestra is so common in Italian homes, and so simple to make, that most restaurants don't even bother putting it on their menus. Minestra can be a broth with one simple ingredient, or it may be an elaborate soup. The base ingredient of minestra is broth. The added ingredients can be a fine pasta, peas, beans, chopped vegetables or any combination of these ingredients. A minestra is simple to fix. If broth is not easily available, a bouillon cube will work. A bouillon cube, 2 or 3 cups of water and a handful of fine pasta make a good minestra in fewer than fifteen minutes.

Meat Broth (Stock)

1 (2 to 3-pound) chicken

2 turkey thighs

1 or 2 beef bones

5 quarts water

3 carrots

2 large onions, each stuck with 2 cloves

3 ribs celery

2 bay leaves

2 tablespoons fresh basil

Put all ingredients in a large pot and boil gently for 3 hours. Skim often during cooking. Chicken may be removed early if it begins to fall apart. At the completion of cooking, discard vegetables and beef bones. After broth has cooled, remove fat from top.

Remember that the broth has to be seasoned with salt and pepper when it is used. Some of the chicken can be boned and put back into a portion of the broth for a delicious chicken soup.

Extra broth may be frozen for future use. Some cooks freeze broth in ice trays and store the broth cubes in plastic bags.

Chicken Broth (Stock)

1 chicken (3 to 4 pounds)

1 onion, stuck with 2 cloves

3 ribs celery

2 carrots

1 cup chopped fresh parsley

4 quarts water

Put all ingredients in a large pot and cook gently for 2 or 3 hours. Skim often if necessary. Remove chicken and bone it for use as desired. After broth has cooled, remove fat from top.

The chicken makes an excellent chicken salad mixed with chopped celery, sweet pickles, hard-cooked eggs and mayonnaise.

Be sure to season the broth when you use it. Some cooks prefer chicken broth without onion and celery.

Vegetable Stock

2 onions, halved

8 ribs celery, cut in large pieces

3 carrots, cut in large pieces

3 quarts water

Put all ingredients in a large pot and cook for 2 hours. Strain and discard vegetables.

Fish Stock

- 1 or 2 pounds throw-away parts of fish
- 1 onion
- 2 carrots
- 3 ribs celery
- 3 quarts water

Put all ingredients in a large pot and boil gently for 2 hours. Strain. You may freeze extra stock.

Simple Minestra with Small Pasta

- 3 cups chicken or beef stock (p.64)
- ¾ cup small pasta (*pastina*), *acini di pepe*, alphabet, *stelline*, etc.
- Salt to taste

Bring broth to a boil. Add pasta and salt. Cook pasta according to directions. Bouillon may be substituted for broth, but do not add salt.

Cinque Terre - the beach

Stracciatella - Italian Egg Drop Soup

- 4 cups chicken broth (p.64)
- 2 eggs
- 1 cup bread crumbs
- ½ cup grated Parmesan
- Zest of ½ lemon
- Salt and pepper

Bring broth to a boil. Beat two eggs with a fork. Add remaining ingredients and mix. The mixture should be a dense fluid. If it is too dense, add either another egg or a little milk.

Remove boiling broth from heat and stir in egg mixture, stirring constantly to avoid lumping. Return to heat for 3 minutes.

Serve with additional Parmesan.

Stracciatella with Spinach

- 6 cups chicken broth (p.64)
- 2 cups chopped fresh spinach
- 2 eggs
- ⅔ cup grated Parmesan
- Zest of ½ lemon
- Salt and pepper
- Juice of ½ lemon

Bring broth to a boil. Add spinach. In a bowl combine eggs, Parmesan, lemon zest, salt and pepper. Mix well.

Remove broth and spinach from heat. Add egg mixture and stir well. Return to heat. Cook 3 minutes more. Add lemon juice and serve.

Minestrone with Lentils and Pig's Feet

2 pig's feet, split

2 onions, chopped

4 tablespoons olive oil

4 cloves garlic, whole

1 cup lentils

1 cup chopped carrots

1 cup diced tomato

1 tablespoon chopped fresh basil

5 cups beef stock (p.64) or water

Salt and pepper

Grated Parmesan

Italians traditionally have lentils (*lenticchie*) and pig's lower leg (*zampone*) on New Year's Day.

In a pot, sauté pig's feet in olive oil, and add all other ingredients except Parmesan. Cover and simmer for 2 hours.

Discard garlic. Break the meat into small pieces. Meat may be served in the soup or separately. Serve with Parmesan.

Pasta Fagioli (Pasta and Beans)

In September, 1996, I had three Italian guests in my home, my third cousin, Marina Calderigi, her husband, Alessio Giamarini , and a friend, Carlo Pavone. Marina and Alessio live in Ancona, Region of the Marche. Carlo is from Pescara, Region of Abruzzo. Carlo is a train engineer, a professional photographer, and an excellent cook. He prepared this dish of Pasta Fagioli.

Carlo prepared the beans, the sauce and the pasta separately. He combined the three after the pasta was cooked *al dente*, making sure that the beans and the sauce were warm when combined with the pasta. When the three elements are combined, the mixture should be slightly soupy. The following recipe will serve 6 people.

Carlo's Pasta Fagioli

For the beans:

1 pound of pinto beans (or borlotti if available)

2 stalks of celery, chopped

4 whole cloves of garlic

1 onion, chopped

1 teaspoon baking soda

Salt

Soak the pinto beans in plenty of water with the baking soda overnight. Drain the beans and combine with other bean ingredients. Cover with water and cook until beans are tender but not soggy.

Drain beans but retain cooking water.

For the sauce:

6 tablespoons olive oil, one for each person

1 onion, chopped

1 stalk celery, chopped

3 cloves garlic, chopped

2 vegetable bouillon cubes

Red pepper flakes

1 large can peeled tomatoes, mashed

Salt to taste

Parsley and basil

Heat olive oil and sauté onion, celery and garlic. Cook about 5 minutes over medium heat. Add tomatoes, bouillon cubes, red pepper flakes and salt. Cook an additional 30 minutes.

For the pasta:

1 pound of short elbow pasta or linguini, broken into pieces about 3 inches long

Cook pasta *al dente* in plenty of salted water.

Drain pasta.

Combine pasta, beans and sauce. If the combination is too dry, add some liquid drained from beans. The Pasta Fagioli should be soupy. Sprinkle with parsley and basil.

Serve Pasta Fagioli in a bowl with ground Parmesan and extra red pepper flakes on the side.

Chickpea Soup

2 cans chickpeas or 1 pound dry, soaked overnight and cooked

½ cup olive oil

1 cup sliced mushrooms

3 or 4 basil leaves

1 cup chopped celery

2 cups diced tomatoes

Salt and pepper

2 cups broth (any kind)

Grated Parmesan

Combine all ingredients and cook for 30 minutes. Serve with Parmesan on the side.

Florence - view from a convent terrace

Crepes in Broth

6 cups chicken broth (p.64)

4 eggs

2 tablespoons milk

2 teaspoons flour

½ teaspoon nutmeg

1 tablespoon chopped parsley

¾ cup grated Parmesan, divided

Salt

Slice of bacon or salt pork

Combine eggs, milk, flour, nutmeg, parsley and ¼ cup Parmesan. Add salt to taste. Whisk well.

Heat a crepe pan and rub bottom with bacon/salt pork. Add 2 tablespoons of egg mixture, tilt pan to cover bottom. Cook briefly until mixture is set, forming a thin pancake. Place crepe on a platter.

Wipe the skillet with a paper towel and repeat process until all batter is used. Sprinkle each crepe with Parmesan and roll the crepe.

Place 2 or 3 crepes in the bottom of individual soup-bowls, pour on hot broth and serve with Parmesan.

Passatelli

7 cups meat broth (p.64)

1 cup Parmesan cheese

½ cup fine bread crumbs

Pinch of nutmeg

Zest of ½ lemon

2 large eggs

Salt and pepper to taste

Bring broth to a gentle boil. Combine all other ingredients in a bowl and form a dough. If the dough is too loose and moist, add more cheese and bread crumbs. If it is too dry to form a dough, add a few drops of water.

If you have a food mill, fit in the disk with large holes. If you do not have a food mill, a ricer may work. Press the mixture through the mill or ricer directly into the boiling broth.

Cook the *passatelli* for 2 or 3 minutes. Allow the soup to rest 3 minutes.

Serve with Parmesan on the side.

Italian-American Version of Minestrone and a Story of the Two Rosetos

Minestrone is one of those dishes the recipe for which depends on the cook's pantry and refrigerator. I found my favorite recipe in Anna Marie Ruggiero's "The Roseto Cuisine Cookbook." Roseto, Pennsylvania, was settled by Italian immigrants from Roseto, Italy. I visited both Rosetos and found their people, attitudes and customs surprisingly alike, well over a hundred years and five generations after the Roseto immigrants settled Pennsylvania in 1882.

I went to Roseto Valfortore with David Trigiani, whose grandfather left there a hundred-plus years ago. We drove the Autostrada from Senigallia, on the Adriatic Coast in Central Italy, to Foggia, Region of Puglia. From Foggia we took the main road toward Lucero on to Alberona. From Alberona we took a winding little road into a desolate area that appeared to be uninhabited. Crossing over what seemed to be the crest of a mountain range, we saw dozens of windmills, the source of power for the area. Then descending past the windmills, we got a glimpse of a tiny village nestled in the valley below. That was Roseto Valfortore, Province of Foggia, Region of Puglia.

Out-of-the-way Italian villages are fascinating, especially if they are unspoiled by tourists. Roseto Valfortore seemed to be that sort of a place. We parked our car in the town's center near a monument that listed Roseto's war dead. The list read like a roster of Roseto, Pennsylvania, residents.

Italians can detect Americans, even if our names are Italian and every drop of our blood is Italian. Even if we speak their language, they can tell we're American by our shoes, the colors we wear and the way we carry ourselves. David and I attracted curious eyes, but I suspect they had an idea who we were. The occasional American tourist in Roseto Valfortore is likely to be from Pennsylvania. Hearing the name Trigiani, their curiosity was satisfied. Everyone in Roseto Valfortore knows Roseto, Pennsylvania. They seemed eager to show us their town.

We saw Roseto's principal church, built with stones that the town's people brought from fields, one by one, as they returned from work every day. We saw the beam used to hang hogs at slaughtering time, fastened into an exterior wall of the church. We saw worshippers at the shrine of St. Phillip Neri. We saw elderly wom-

Puglia - Roseto, cemetery chapel

Roseto
Little Church near Cemetery   6/19/00

en and men who seemed to belong to a time and place long past. What impressed us most was the reflection of Roseto, Pennsylvania.

Roseto, U.S.A., is certainly not remote, although the first Italian settlers may have thought so when they came in 1882 to work in Pennsylvania's slate quarries. The new Roseto sits in the shadow of the Pocono Mountains on the eastern edge of Pennsylvania, 80 miles from Philadelphia and 90 miles from New York City. The little borough, the population of which is under 2000, still maintains its Italian heritage, and in certain respects, its Italian way of life. Although just a half of Roseto's present population can boast of Italian ancestry, the town has a definite old-world flavor. You can still get bread stuffed with anchovy and pepperoni at Le Donne's Bakery on Garibaldi Avenue, home of the original tomato pie. At Ruggiero's Market you can get anything you need for your Italian cuisine and inhale the aromas of old Roseto. When I visited the Market, Anna Marie Ruggiero gave me a copy of her cookbook. This is her recipe for minestrone.

Anna Marie Ruggiero's Minestrone

2 tablespoons olive oil

1 onion, chopped

1 clove garlic, minced

2 ripe tomatoes, peeled and mashed

1 cup chopped celery, including leaves

½ cup chopped parsley

¼ cup chopped basil

2 potatoes, cubed

1 cup cut green beans

1 carrot, chopped

1 cup Swiss chard, finely sliced

1 cup chickpeas

2 quarts beef broth

Salt and pepper

8 ounces short pasta

Heat oil in large pot. Sauté onion and garlic. Add tomatoes, celery, parsley and basil. Cook 5 minutes.

Add 1 cup water and simmer 5 minutes. Add remaining ingredients and cook until tender (about 15 minutes). Season to taste.

Cook pasta, any short pasta such as small shells, according to directions. Drain and add to soup with hot broth.

Sunset - Collage

An Italian Wedding

The wedding is the apex of Italian celebration, an occasion for sumptuous spreads of food and beverage, music, dance and pranks. Francesca and Simone's[1] wedding was typically Italian, but extraordinary, at least in the eyes of an American.

Francesca and Simone are a beautiful couple, about thirty years old and full of life. Francesca is tall, thin, blonde, blue eyed and striking in appearance. She's a dental hygienist. Simone is handsome, somewhat shy and has a mind of his own. He's a talented computer technician and works in his family's advertising-printing business. In his off-time he plays African-Caribbean drums with a local band. He's my cousin Vanda's grandson. The couple were engaged, *fidanzati*, for over fourteen years. Long engagements are ordinary for Italians. They usually put off marriage until they are settled in a job and financially able to set up house, about thirty years old or older.

The wedding was in the church of San Pietro Apostolo in Montemarciano, Province of Ancona. It was scheduled for 4:30 in the afternoon. The principal decoration for the wedding was red peppers, the *peperoncino*. Simone has relatives in Naples, where the red pepper symbolizes good fortune, *buona fortuna*. On each side of the front door of the church there were two large olive trees in huge pots and little pots of red peppers surrounded the trunks of the olive trees. Inside the church a pot of red peppers, grapevines and a white bow adorned the aisle-end of every fourth pew. The area around the altar was decorated with

[1]Francesca Giacomelli and Simone Manservigi

five large urns containing white gladiolas and at the base of the gladiolas were small pots of red peppers. The front of the altar and the wedding pre-dieux were decorated with grapevines, and resting on the pre-dieux was the bride's bouquet of white roses surrounded with red peppers and green leaves that looked like bay leaves. The decoration theme was definitely "good fortune." Simone said the grapevines stood for prosperity.

Peppers For Good Fortune

It was a hot Saturday afternoon. Several elderly men sat across the street from the church in front of the Bar Centrale and the Ristorante Portico. Two or three were weathering the heat in their undershirts. They are undoubtedly there every day, but that afternoon they seemed to delight in the wedding festivities.

Guests began to arrive at about 4:15. It seemed no one wanted to get out into the heat earlier than necessary. The first to arrive were the photographers, three or four. They positioned themselves at strategic places outside the church so they would miss nothing. Guests were dressed in extremes, elegant to ultra-casual. One of the first men to arrive wore jeans and carried a coat draped over his arm. Another had a collarless shirt, tail out, and reddish trousers. One young man arrived shirtless and put on an orange T-shirt as he got out of his car. The prize for casual dress went to the young man in white pedal-pushers and a T-shirt with *Baci e Abbracci* (Kisses and Hugs) written in large letters on the back. Sara Marinelli, cousin of the groom, wore a tight-fitting black outfit, laced in front like an outside corset, with stocking clips hanging on each side. One automobile was stuffed with balloons to be used for one of the pranks later that evening. The bride's mother arrived alone.

Ordinarily the Italian groom arrives at the church accompanied by his mother and carrying the bride's bouquet. Simone is not ordinary. He

The Bride   CANONICI

arrived in a sleek, silver, convertible Alfa Romeo chauffeured by a friend, horn blowing as he approached the church. Like all Italian weddings, the cars bearing the spouses and their families were elegantly decorated with white ribbon. At the sight of the groom everyone shouted and applauded. Simone looked handsomely stunning, his hair slightly spiked, a second-day beard, and a ring prominently displayed at the top of his left ear. He wore a white suit, open collar Elvis-style shirt, tight trouser legs and white, very pointed, alligator-skin shoes without socks. His black belt added accent to his white attire and his boutonniere of red peppers positioned him into the theme of his wedding. I'm sure everyone present thought "This is Simone" (*Ecco Simone*).

At 4:30 the bride was not in sight. No one seemed concerned, not even the priest, at the front door prepared to greet the wedding party. At 4:45 there was another blast of car horns and a thunder of shouting and applauding. The bride and her father, Giorgio Giacomelli, were speedily chauffeured to the front steps of the church.

The back door opened and Francesca took a leap from the automobile onto the church steps, waving and throwing kisses to the crowd of guests as she glided up the church steps to meet Simone. They embraced. Francesca was strikingly beautiful, her veil flowing over her long blonde hair done in corn-rows. Simone described her hairdo as *freeze*. She wore a short pearled blouse, a hip-hugging mini skirt, a long detachable train, silver high heels, very high, with silver straps around her ankles. I approached to kiss her, but she shielded her face and gently asked me to wait. Her perfect make-up was not to be disturbed.

Once the bride had arrived, the procession began to form led by the priest, Don Giuseppe; then came the ring bearers -- a girl and a boy, the groom and his mother, the bride and her father. Then came the four witnesses: the groom's brother, Lorenzo and his girlfriend, Benedetta, and two brothers of the bride's mother. There were no bridesmaids or groomsmen. The groom's father, the bride's mother and other close family members came next. Finally, guests filed into church.

Once at the altar, Simone was handed a taper. He lit the Paschal candle and one of two candles on the altar. Francesca lit the other. The liturgy lacked the orderly flow that I was accustomed to. Photographers wandered freely to get the best shots possible. Some guests moved around the church and talked. The public address system was not working, making it difficult to hear the readings. The Responsorial Psalm was omitted.

Don Giuseppe wore green vestments. White is ordinarily used for weddings. But who am I to say that Simone's wedding was extraordinary; and who am I to pass judgment on the liturgy of the Nuptial Mass? After all, the Italians have been doing Catholic church weddings for nearly 2000 years.

Spouses and witnesses signed various books and documents. The Nuptial Mass was concluded and the organist began the recessional. I was positioned to take pictures of the spouses leaving the church, but to my surprise, there was no recessional. Francesca and Simone turned, facing their guests, family and friends, and everyone in the church made their way forward to kiss the newlyweds on both cheeks.

After greeting the *sposi*, guests waited on the steps outside the front door of the church. Francesca and Simone finally appeared, shielding their faces from a shower of rice. Some poured rice from bags. Covered with rice, the newlyweds continued greeting guests, when to everyone's surprise, except the bride's father, a thirty-piece band, its members dressed in white trousers and sky blue shirts, came blasting around the corner playing jubilant wedding music. They concluded with the Italian "best wishes" song, *Tanti Auguri a Te*, to the tune of "Happy Birthday." While the band played and guests applauded, Simone and his bride whisked away in their silver convertible Alfa Romeo.

After the church ceremony, Italian newlyweds traditionally go to some special place for photographs, some historical place or some local nature area. Francesca and Simone chose a recently harvested wheat field with rolled bales of golden-colored hay and historical Fosombrone, a medieval village near the place they had chosen for their wedding dinner.

While the *sposi* took pictures, we guests made our way to the Palazzino Sabatelli in the area of San Ippolito, Province of Pesaro, location of the dinner. The Palazzino was once the hunting lodge of some wealthy family. Besides spacious living quarters, there's a chapel and several other buildings. Now there's also a swimming pool. Francesca and Simone spent their wedding night there, what was left of the night after the party.

While guests arrived and while we waited for the newlyweds, light *antipasti* and champagne were served at various locations on the grounds: fried stuffed olives, encrusted zucchini, squash blossoms, fried cauliflower and eggplant, spinach-stuffed pastry and small squares of light pizza.

Live music resounded from the pool area to which we were directed for a sumptuous buffet of heavier *antipasti* after the arrival of Francesca and Simone. I cannot begin to name all the hors d'oeuvres laid out on tables the whole length and width of the pool area: salmon, sea bass, muscles, clams and so many others. The menu listed the buffet as *Gran Buffet di Antipasti della Villa con Tesori dell 'Adriatico* (The Great Buffet of the Villa's Hors d'oeuvres and Adriatic Treasures).

The buffet of *antipasti* would have been more than enough food for a grand dinner, but it was just the beginning. We then moved to the main dining hall for dinner. Tables were elegantly set, enough places for about 250 guests. Each place had a favor consisting of *confetti* (candy-coated almonds), nicely wrapped in brown and tied with a hemp cord with a couple of red peppers fastened on top.

I was seated next to my 95-year-old cousin, Vanda, who was guarding her little black purse, holding on as if she thought the purse might slip away any moment. For me, the highlight of the evening was when Vanda leaned toward me and whispered, "I have the money to pay for this wedding dinner. They gave me the money to watch." Vanda looked lovely. Her hair had a light tint, and she wore a dark blue outfit with white trimmings. She told me she was living to see her grandchildren wedded. Now two out of three - Francesco and Simone - were married, and Lorenzo would marry the following summer.

Dinner consisted of linguine of the house with a cherry tomato and porcini mushroom sauce, tagliatelle with asparagus tips, encrusted veal, beef filet on a bed of rucola and small tomatoes, all accompanied by mixed vegetables. Toward the end of the meal the groom's friends performed a few pranks. Then lighted sparklers were handed out and two husky young men brought in the cake, about a yard or more in diameter. As the cake was cut, music played and a snake dance formed, led by Bruno, a little man with red trousers, Simone's relative from Naples.

I left at 1:30 a.m., but the party continued into the morning. After dinner the celebration moved to another location where there was dancing and a buffet of desserts, fruit, gelato and crepes. Cousin Vanda stayed until the end, about 4:00 a.m.

Secondi
Main Dishes

Venice - Burano

Berard
4/22/00

Chicken Croquettes

Béchamel sauce

2 eggs, divided

Cooked chicken, ground or finely chopped

Parmesan cheese

Salt and pepper

Nutmeg

Flour

Bread crumbs

Butter

Vegetable oil

Prepare béchamel sauce according to recipe on page 152. When béchamel sauce is ready, mix 1 egg into the sauce and allow to cool.

Mix chicken, Parmesan cheese, salt and pepper to taste, nutmeg and sufficient béchamel to form a thick consistency. Form mixture into croquettes.

For batter, lightly beat 1 egg and add salt. Dredge croquettes in flour, egg batter and finally in bread crumbs. Fry croquettes in butter or plenty vegetable oil.

Region: Emilia Romagna

Chicken with Mushrooms and Potatoes

1 chicken, cut into serving pieces

1 pound potatoes, peeled and sliced

2 cups tomatoes, peeled and mashed

2 cups mushrooms, cleaned with cloth, stems halved and mushrooms left intact

3 tablespoons butter

2 small fresh onions, cut into wedges; or 1 small onion, wedged in eighths

2 cloves garlic, chopped

½ cup finely chopped parsley

Pinch of marjoram

1 tablespoon chopped basil

½ cup olive oil, divided

1 cup dry white wine

Salt and pepper

Heat 2 tablespoons of olive oil in a deep skillet. Add chicken and brown on all sides. Add onions and allow to turn golden. Then add wine and allow it to evaporate. Add tomatoes, parsley, basil, marjoram, salt and pepper. Cook over moderate heat for 1 hour.

In the meantime, heat the remaining olive oil in a saucepan, preferably stoneware, and add garlic, mushrooms and potatoes. Add salt to taste and cook about 35 minutes.

Put the chicken on a serving dish and surround it with mushrooms and potatoes. Serve immediately.

Rome-Via Veneto

Excelsior Hotel -Rome
next to Am. Embassy

Chicken with Olives and Tomatoes

- 1 chicken, cut into serving pieces
- 1 cup pitted green olives
- 2 cups tomato puree
- 6 anchovy fillets, mashed into paste
- ½ cup olive oil
- 1 clove garlic, crushed and mashed into paste
- ½ cup parsley, chopped
- **Salt and pepper**

In a deep skillet or large saucepan, heat oil. Add chicken, salt and pepper. Brown pieces of chicken on all sides. Remove chicken and keep warm.

Put anchovy, garlic and tomato puree in the same pan and cook for 10 minutes. Scrape bottom and sides of pan with wooden spoon. Stir well.

Return chicken to the pan. Add olives, bring to a boil and add 2 tablespoons of water. Cover and continue cooking for 15 minutes.

Place chicken on a serving dish and sprinkle with parsley. Serve immediately.

Chicken Roman Style

1 chicken, cut into serving pieces

2 tablespoons butter

2 tablespoons olive oil

1 cup ham or *prosciutto*, diced

1 clove garlic, chopped

1 cup dry white wine

Salt and pepper

2 peppers, red, yellow or green, cut in strips

Brown chicken in olive oil and butter with ham/*prosciutto* and garlic. When chicken begins to brown, add wine, salt and pepper. Allow the wine to evaporate over high heat.

Lower heat, add peppers, cover and cook for at least 30 minutes longer. Keep the bottom of the pan moist. If sauce becomes too dense, add hot stock or water. Serve chicken with sauce.

Region: Lazio

Florence from Grand Hotel

Chicken Calabrese

1 tender chicken, cut into serving pieces

2 tablespoons olive oil

2 tablespoons butter

1 cup dry white wine

1 cup white vinegar

4 cloves garlic

2 cups diced tomatoes

1 tablespoon chopped rosemary

1 tablespoon chopped sage

1 teaspoon oregano

1 tablespoon capers

Salt and pepper

Brown the chicken on all sides in olive oil and butter.

In a blender mix wine, vinegar, garlic, tomatoes, rosemary, sage, oregano, capers, salt and pepper. Pour mixture over chicken. Cover and bring to a boil.

Uncover and cook over low to moderate heat for 30 minutes. If excess liquid remains at conclusion of cooking, remove chicken and turn up heat to reduce liquid.

Place chicken in a serving platter. Pour sauce over chicken and serve.

Mrs. Lisa Olmi's Stuffed Chicken

Stuffed chicken was a Sunday special in most Italian-American homes. This recipe was undoubtedly brought to America from the Marche Region by Lisa Sandroni Olmi's family.

Use mixture prepared for Mrs. Olmi's Meat Balls (p.23). Add sautéed chicken livers. Stuff chicken. Sew opening and fasten legs. Rub outside of chicken with olive oil. Season with salt and pepper. Sprinkle with paprika. Bake in oven preheated to 350°.

Marinated Beef

1½ pounds beef, cut into 1½-inch pieces

Sea salt

1 cup vinegar

4 cups hearty red wine

1 clove garlic, finely chopped

2 cups celery, chopped

6 or 8 clove stems

1 bay leaf

1 onion, chopped

4 tablespoons olive oil

Cover meat with sea salt and allow to rest in a cool place overnight. In the morning, wash the meat with vinegar.

Put the meat in a bowl with the wine, garlic, celery, cloves and bay leaf. Allow to marinate for 24 hours.

Sauté onion in olive oil until transparent. Add meat, salt and pepper. Moisten the meat with some of the marinade, cover and cook over moderate heat for 1 hour.

Region: Calabria

Roast Beef Seasoned with Garlic and Anchovy

2 pounds tender beef

2 or 3 cloves garlic, halved

8 anchovy fillets, divided

4 tablespoons butter

Oregano

2 cups dry white wine

Juice of 1 lemon

Salt and pepper

With a narrow knife, pierce the meat deeply in several places. With your finger force a piece of garlic and a piece of 4 anchovies into each piercing.

Melt the butter in a roasting pan or Dutch oven and brown meat on all sides.

Chop the remaining 4 anchovy fillets and add them to the meat. Add the oregano, wine and lemon juice, and continue cooking over low heat. Turn and moisten the meat from time to time. The meat should cook slowly until it is very tender and anchovies are completely dissolved.

Region: Calabria

Pork Loin with Raspberry Sauce

3-pound pork loin

3 cups raspberries

1 cup sugar (or Splenda)

Olive oil

4 tablespoons butter

Beef stock or bouillon

Sage

Rosemary

Salt and pepper to taste

Tie pork loin with kitchen twine so that it holds its form. Apply salt and pepper. Put loin in a baking dish or pan with olive oil, butter, sage and rosemary. Set oven to 400° and bake for 1 hour, basting from time to time with hot beef stock.

While the pork is baking, wash the raspberries and allow them to dry. Place raspberries in a saucepan with sugar and cook over moderate heat for about 30 minutes, stirring constantly. Strain the sauce and serve it hot with sliced roasted pork loin.

Region: Friuli Venezia Giulia

Venice

Pork Ribs in Tomato Sauce

21 pieces of pork ribs

½ pound sausage, cut into bite-size pieces

4 tablespoons butter

2 tablespoons olive oil

1 cup dry white wine

1 onion, sliced

1 carrot, chopped

2 cloves garlic, finely chopped

½ cup chopped parsley

1 cup chopped celery

3 cups sliced tomatoes

Salt and pepper

Fry the onion in oil and butter until lightly golden. Add celery, carrot, garlic and parsley. Cook for 5 minutes. Add ribs, salt, pepper and wine. Cook over moderate heat for 10 minutes to reduce liquid. Then cover, lower heat and cook for 30 minutes.

Add tomatoes and sausage. Continue cooking for 20 minutes more. Then serve ribs with sauce and fresh bread for sopping. This dish is accompanied well by polenta or mashed potatoes.

Region: Lazio

The Dancing Pines

3-19-02

Pork Stew with Red Peppers (Spezzatino di Maiale)

For 4 servings:

1½ **pounds pork loin**

3 **red peppers (or red and yellow)**

4 **tablespoons butter**

1 **bay leaf**

1 **garlic clove, chopped**

½ **cup chopped parsley**

Chopped thyme

2 **tablespoons flour**

Stock

Salt and pepper

Clean peppers and cut into strips. Cut pork loin into chunks about 1 to 1½ inches square. Season with salt and freshly ground pepper. Heat butter in large pan. Brown pork over high heat, stirring constantly. After about 10 minutes, drain off fat and stir in 2 tablespoons flour.

When flour turns golden, add bay leaf and a mixture of garlic, parsley and thyme. Cover with stock and cook over low heat for 1 hour, adding more stock if contents become too thick or too dry.

When meat is just about cooked, add peppers and cook for 20 minutes more. Serve from cooking pan.

Senigallia - restoration of the Rotonda

Lamb with Wild Fennel

For 4 servings:

4 large lamb chops or 8 very small

¼ cup chopped rosemary

1 clove garlic, finely chopped

¼ cup finely chopped wild fennel

1 cup dry white wine

½ cup olive oil

Salt and pepper

2 tablespoons butter

Italians like to chop their herbs all together. They call the chopped mixture a *trito*.

Heat the olive oil and butter and cook the rosemary, garlic and fennel for 5 minutes over low heat. Add the meat and apply salt and pepper. When the meat has browned on both sides, add the wine, cover and continue cooking for 45 minutes to 1 hour.

Try serving this lamb dish with roasted new potatoes and buttered green peas.

Region: The Marche

Osso Buco with Gremolata Sauce

Gremolata Sauce (p.152)

4 pieces veal shank, about 3 inches thick

Flour

3 tablespoons olive oil

3 whole garlic cloves

1 medium onion, finely chopped

½ cup chopped carrot

1 tablespoon basil

Salt and pepper

1 cup dry white wine

2 cups tomato puree

2 tablespoons butter

Preheat oven to 400°.

Dredge veal in flour. Heat oil in a wide skillet. Add veal and cook, uncovered, over medium heat. Lightly brown shanks on both sides.

Add garlic, onion, carrot, basil, salt and pepper. When onion turns lightly golden, add wine, cover and lower heat. Simmer for 8 to 10 minutes, stirring often. Add tomatoes and butter. Cover and continue simmering for 10 minutes longer.

Place skillet in oven and bake at 400° 30 minutes. Lower heat to 350° and bake 30 minutes more.

Prepare the gremolata. Scatter gremolata over shanks and serve with Risotto Milanese (p.56).

Stuffed Veal Cutlets

For 4 servings:

4 veal cutlets, preferably thick, with bone

½ pound sausage, freed of casing

¼ pound ham

¼ pound cooked chicken

1 cup chopped parsley

2 eggs, lightly beaten

Bread crumbs

Salt

Butter for frying

Grind the ham and chicken and mix with sausage, chopped parsley and a little salt to taste. Open each cutlet, leaving one side not cut all the way through. Beat each side of the cutlet to extend its size. Divide stuffing into four parts and put a portion on one side of each cutlet. Close each cutlet and fasten with a toothpick or two.

Salt the cutlets and pass each through the egg wash and then through the bread crumbs. Brown the stuffed cutlets in butter over moderate heat. Allow the cutlets to cook all the way through. The cutlets may be baked, but be sure to butter them on both sides. Pork chops may be substituted for veal cutlets.

The meat may be served with a Parmesan risotto, buttered green peas, zucchini or fried potatoes.

Fried Cutlets

The cutlets may be veal, beef, lamb, pork, chicken or turkey.

Cutlets, in quantity desired

For the batter:

2 eggs, lightly beaten

Juice of 1 lemon

¾ cup Parmesan cheese

½ cup milk

Pinch of nutmeg

Salt and pepper

Bread crumbs

Vegetable oil for frying

Combine all the ingredients for the batter and mix well. Marinate the cutlets in the batter for about 1 hour. Then coat the cutlets with fine bread crumbs.

Fry the cutlets in vegetable oil until golden on both sides.

Region: Emilia Romagna

Venice - Gondolas

Three pines

Veal Marsala by Italian-Americans

This recipe for Veal Marsala, contributed by Charles Burckel and his wife, Regina Ortolano, is genuinely Italian. Regina took us to the home where her grandmother lived in Caccamo, near Palermo, Sicily.

2 teaspoons butter, divided

Salt, pepper, flour

4 slices baby, white veal scallops

Sauce:

1 tablespoon butter

1 tablespoon chopped onion

¼ teaspoon chopped garlic

5 medium-large mushrooms, sliced

¼ cup dry Marsala

¼ cup dry white wine

½ cup veal demi-glacé

¼ teaspoon salt

Pinch of black pepper

Dust veal scallops very lightly with salt, pepper and flour. Heat skillet to high temperature. Add half of butter and swirl around. Sauté veal for 45 seconds on each side. Remove from skillet and keep warm. Add the remaining butter and finish sautéing the veal.

Make the sauce in the same skillet, incorporating veal juices. Heat the butter in the skillet until it bubbles. Add onions and garlic. Sauté until transparent. Add mushrooms and sauté until mushrooms are tender. Add Marsala and white wine and bring to a boil. Cook for 2 minutes, stirring occasionally. Add demi-glacé, return to a boil and add salt and pepper to taste. Sauce will still be rather light in consistency and will have the distinct flavor echoes of the Marsala.

Sauce can be ladled over the sautéed veal or the veal can be put in the sauce for a thicker consistency.

Sailboat in the night

Veal (or Beef) Rolls In Tomato Sauce

1½-pound veal rump (or beef tenderloin), thinly sliced and pounded

¼ pound *prosciutto* (or ham), finely chopped

2 cloves garlic, 1 finely chopped, 1 left whole

½ cup chopped parsley

½ cup chopped basil

Salt and pepper

2 cups tomato puree

6 tablespoons olive oil, divided

1 cup dry white wine

Spread the pounded slices of meat on a counter. Mix the *prosciutto*/ham, 1 clove chopped garlic, parsley, basil, salt and pepper. Spread some of the mixture on each slice of meat. Roll and fasten each slice with a toothpick.

Heat 3 tablespoons olive oil in a pan. Sauté the whole garlic clove until light golden. Remove the garlic and add tomatoes. Add salt and pepper. Cook for 30 minutes. The sauce should thicken.

In a pan, preferably stoneware, heat the remaining 3 tablespoons oil and brown meat rolls. Add a cup of wine and allow it to evaporate. Pour in the tomato puree and continue cooking over low heat for 15 or 20 minutes. The meat rolls may be breaded by dredging them through flour, a beaten egg and bread crumbs.

Grilled Breaded Cutlets

4 veal cutlets

Crisco (*Strutto*)

Bread crumbs

Oregano

Salt and pepper

Veal is plentiful in Italy. Consequently Italians use much more veal than Americans. This dish can be prepared with chicken, turkey or beef.

Pound the cutlets. Smear Crisco lightly over cutlets and then dredge through bread crumbs seasoned with oregano, salt and pepper.

Cook until golden on a very hot grill.

Region: Sicily

Grilled Meat Rolls and Onions

1 pound veal rump, sliced thinly and pounded (chicken, beef, pork or turkey may be substituted for veal)

¼ pound Provolone cheese, cut in small pieces

¾ cup raisins, soaked in warm water

½ cup pine nuts

2 cups bread crumbs

Several bay leaves

Salt and pepper

2 onions, cut into pieces

Olive oil

In a skillet heat a little olive oil and brown bread crumbs. Allow bread crumbs to cool. Combine bread crumbs, provolone, raisins, pine nuts, salt and pepper. Mix well.

Put a heaping tablespoon of the mixture on each slice of meat and wrap the meat to form a roll. Tie each roll with a string.

Thread the rolls, bay leaves and pieces of onion onto a skewer. Cook on a very hot grill. Baste with a little oil or stock.

Region: Sicily

Grilled Beef Rolls and Peppers

1+ pound tender beef (or pork), thinly sliced and pounded

1 cup chopped *prosciutto* or ham

Salt and pepper

2 cloves garlic, chopped

½ cup chopped parsley

2 cups bread crumbs, moistened with stock, bouillon or water, squeeze to remove excess liquid

1 cup grated Parmesan

5 tablespoons butter

Firm bread, cut into pieces for skewering

Peppers, any color, cut into pieces for skewering

Apply salt and pepper to pounded slices of meat. Combine garlic, parsley, bread crumbs, *prosciutto*/ham, Parmesan, salt and pepper. Mix well.

Put about a tablespoon of filling on each slice of meat. Roll each slice of meat with filling and tie with a string.

Alternate meat rolls, peppers and bread on skewers. Cook on hot grill, basting with melted butter, stock or olive oil. Turn at least twice while cooking. Serve with a mixed salad.

Region: Campania

Sorrento from our hotel

Grilled Beef Steaks Basted with Herbs (Salmoriglia)

Tender beef steaks, 1/2-inch thick

1 clove garlic, minced or mashed into paste

1 stem fresh rosemary or oregano

3 tablespoons dry oregano

3 tablespoons water

1 tablespoon olive oil

Prepare the baste (*salmoriglia*). Combine garlic, oregano, water and olive oil. Beat with a fork to mix well.

Cook the steaks on a grill or grilling pan. While grilling, baste the meat with the *salmoriglia* using the oregano or the rosemary branch. Salt during the final minute of cooking.

The *salmoriglia* is also used for basting fish on the grill.

Region: Calabria

Meat Cooked alla Pizzaiola

6 or 8 slices tender veal or beef, pounded

2 cloves garlic, sliced

5 tablespoons olive oil, divided

1 small can diced tomatoes or, preferably, 2 cups fresh tomatoes, peeled

1 cup dry white wine

Plenty of oregano

Salt and pepper to taste

Optional: 2 tablespoons butter

It is the oregano that gives this dish its distinctive flavor.

Heat 2 tablespoons olive oil in a deep skillet. Sauté garlic until lightly golden. Remove garlic and add slices of pounded meat. Brown the slices on both sides. Remove the meat from the skillet, but keep it warm.

Add the remaining 3 tablespoons olive oil to the skillet. You may also add butter. Heat the oil. Add tomatoes, salt, pepper and a generous sprinkling of oregano. Cook over medium heat for 10 minutes. Add wine and cook 10 additional minutes. Then add the meat slices to the sauce and cook for 5 minutes.

Serve with boiled, peeled potatoes, sliced and dressed with salt, pepper, parsley and olive oil.

Region: Campania

Stew with Goat and Potatoes

6 tablespoons olive oil

2 pounds goat, not more than 40 days old, preferably leg or shoulder, cut into 1 1/2-inch pieces

1 pound potatoes, peeled and cut into large pieces

1 large can tomatoes, not drained

2 onions, sliced

1 teaspoon oregano

Salt and pepper

In a large baking pan, combine olive oil, goat meat, potatoes, tomatoes and onions. Season with oregano, salt and pepper. Cover and bake at 400°, stirring from time to time. Cook until meat is tender.

Region: Puglia

Goulash

For 6 servings:

1/2 pound lean beef, cut into bite-size pieces

2 onions, chopped

1 clove garlic, finely chopped

1 tablespoon tomato paste

2 potatoes, cut into bite-size pieces

1 teaspoon paprika

2 tablespoons butter

2 tablespoons olive oil

Salt

1 bay leaf

Dash of cumin

Dash of marjoram

Zest of 1 lemon

Cook onion and garlic in oil and butter until onion is transparent. Add meat, paprika and tomato paste. Cook for 15 minutes. Then sprinkle lightly with flour. Add 1 1/2 quarts water. Salt to taste and continue cooking until meat is almost tender. Then add potatoes. When the potatoes are cooked, add bay leaf, lemon zest, cumin and marjoram. Cook about 5 minutes longer and serve.

Region: Trentino Alto Adige

Oxtail alla Romana

2 pounds oxtail, cut in 1 1/2 to 2-inch pieces

5 tablespoons lard (Crisco)

3 cloves garlic, crushed well

1 onion, chopped

1 cup dry white wine

1 bay leaf

Red pepper flakes to taste

3 cups chopped tomatoes

6 ribs celery, chopped

Stock

Salt and pepper

In a heavy skillet heat lard and fry oxtail with onion, garlic, bay leaf and red pepper flakes. Season with salt and pepper. Cook for 30 minutes. Add wine. When wine has evaporated, add tomatoes and chopped celery. Cover and cook for about 2 hours. Check from time to time. Keep sauce fluid with stock.

The Old Timers used to add raisins, pine nuts and cinnamon. With this dish you may serve boiled potatoes and carrots. Slice potatoes and carrots. Then season with salt, olive oil and parsley.

Region: Lazio

Treasures in Umbria

Umbria is a small region in the very center of Italy, sandwiched by the regions of Lazio, The Marche and Tuscany. Tucked away in the Apennine Mountains, its treasures are protected from the invasion of American tourists, except for Assisi, home of St. Francis, and Perugia, known for its university and chocolates. There are at least three other towns in Umbria that I like, Deruta, Gubbio and Norcia; and I like the drive through Umbria. Although it is one of the few regions of Italy that does not border on a sea, it has beautiful lakes and mountains just tall enough to preserve a lush green mantle.

Gubbio is located in the northeastern corner of Umbria, on the first slope of Mt. Ingino, a small mountain of the Apennines. It is a medieval town with Gothic architecture and narrow streets that circle the mountain to the top level, where the twelfth century Cathedral (*Duomo*) and administrative buildings are perched. The town's grey stone gives it an austere look.

When you go to Gubbio, you will park in the square near the market area. Be sure to notice the covered opening above the market. That's where the town's sheep-growers used to hang their wool to dry.

In Gubbio I never fail to visit Assunta Rossi, a potter whose shop is

Basilica of St. Francis

assisi 5-24-06 - from Aug

at the top of the incline on the right side of the market. Her black pottery, like much pottery in Gubbio's many shops, is not functional but beautiful. Widowed as a young mother, Assunta educated with her craft two sons, an architect and a physician. She tells my American traveling companions that she has repeatedly asked me to take her to America, but I refuse to heed her request.

Many of Gubbio's shops were fourteenth and fifteenth-century dwellings of wealthy merchants. The houses have a main door and a narrower door fronting on the street, usually just a few inches from the main entrance and a foot or so above the street level. The smaller door is called *porta dei morti* (door of the dead), because it was used only to remove bodies of the dead from the house. Assunta Rossi told me this and her story is supported by written accounts.

Gubbio is known for its Palio, the *Corsa dei Ceri* (Candle Race) held on May 15 every year. If you are in Gubbio about that time, you will see banners throughout the town in colors of the three competing teams, yellow, blue and black. Each team carries the statue of its patron saint mounted on a wooden octagonal frame about 30-feet tall and weighing about a thousand pounds. Teams race from the main square at the foot of the slope up the mountainside through spiraling streets to the Cathedral at the top level.

Assisi - Basilica of S. Francis

When I look down from the Cathedral square onto Gubbio's clay rooftops and wheat fields beyond the town, I'm taken back to medieval times when small city-states of the area battled one another. I'm taken back to the Gubbio of Francis' time and realize how fortunate I am to be walking in the footsteps of the Great Saint from neighboring Assisi.

Norcia is a town in southeastern Umbria, in a plain abutting the Sibylline Mountains, a sub-range of the Apennines. The area is known for its clean air and lush mountain scenery. It is a paradise for mountain hikers and for hunters of wild boar.

Norcia is known for its hams, sausage and other preserved meats made from wild boar and pork; and the people of Norcia were known in times past for their meat preservation skills. Before the invention of the meat grinder, Norcians traveled from house to house in neighboring regions to process pork for farmers. They would chop the meat and season it just right for preservation before it was put into casings, which consisted of cleaned hog's intestines. Their pay was usually a portion of the meat. Meat processors came to be called *norcini*, and even today a place that sells *salumi* is sometimes called a *norcineria*, so named for Norcia. There is nothing quite like a plate of cold cuts and a glass of red wine at one of Norcia's sidewalk cafés.

Sausage, Peppers and Potatoes

1 large potato or 2 small potatoes, cut into bite-size pieces

1 pound tomatoes, peeled and cut into large pieces

1 large onion, thickly sliced

3 peppers, any color, cut into strips

1 pound sausage in short links, or long links cut in half

Salt and pepper

Olive oil

In a large skillet, preferably stoneware, cook onion in olive oil until golden.

Add sausage and cook 10 minutes. Add tomatoes, potatoes, peppers and a cup or more of water if needed to form a light sauce. Wine may be added instead of water, or a combination of wine and water. Cover and cook until the vegetables are cooked and a dense sauce forms. Season with salt and pepper. The potatoes may be excluded.

Region: Emilia Romagna

Fried Sausage

Needless to say, for a truly Italian dish, Italian sausage should be used for this and any other dish that calls for sausage.

For 4 servings:

1 to 2 pounds pork sausage

Water or wine

Cut sausage into 1½ to 2-inch pieces and prick the casing several times with a fork. Place the pieces of sausage in a skillet in a single layer. Add about ½ inch of water in the bottom of the pan. Bring to a low boil and continue cooking over low heat. Turn frequently and continue

pricking the casing of the sausage to release grease. When the interior of the sausage is cooked and all the water evaporated, continue cooking in the sausage's own grease until the pieces are well browned.

Wine may be used instead of water, either red or white. For a one-dish meal, add peppers cut into strips, any color. Sauté peppers in another skillet and add to sausage after the water (or wine) has evaporated.

Region: Sicily

Rabbit with Peppers

1 rabbit, cut into serving pieces

3 peppers, any color, cut into strips

3 tablespoons butter

3 tablespoons olive oil

2 cups stock or bouillon

3 anchovy fillets

4 tablespoons white vinegar

1 clove garlic, chopped

1 bay leaf

1 tablespoon chopped rosemary

Salt

Melt butter in a deep skillet. Add garlic, rosemary and rabbit pieces. Brown the rabbit and allow it to cook about 10 minutes. Adjust salt; add bay leaf and stock. Cook for at least 1 hour.

In the meantime, heat oil in another skillet and add anchovy, vinegar and peppers. Adjust for salt and cook on low heat for about 30 minutes.

About 10 minutes before the rabbit is removed from heat, add the peppers. Serve rabbit and peppers together.

Tagliatelle with Wild Rabbit

Valle d'Aosta, Italy's smallest and least populated region, is in the Alps at the country's northern border. The region has a strong French influence in culture and cuisine and is bilingual with both Italian and French taught in schools and at home. Valle d'Aosta attracts tourists in winter and summer. The Alpine forest of the region is a hunter's paradise, and its spacious pastures are rich with cattle, hogs, sheep and goats. Valle d'Aosta's cuisine celebrates its local products: game, all kinds of meat, mushrooms, fruits and wine.

1 wild rabbit

Tagliatelle, preferably fresh

1/2 pound mushrooms, sliced

3 tablespoons butter

1 onion, half thinly sliced, half chopped

2 cloves garlic, crushed and divided

1 bay leaf

1 carrot, chopped

1 rib celery, chopped

3+ cups dry red wine

2 tablespoons flour

Salt and pepper

Olive oil

Cut rabbit into serving pieces and put into a deep pan with the thinly sliced onion, 1 clove garlic, bay leaf, celery, pepper and salt. Cover all ingredients with wine and allow to marinate for 3 or 4 hours, turning meat from time to time.

In a deep skillet, melt butter. Add the chopped onion and chopped carrot. Cook until onion is lightly golden. Add pieces of rabbit and brown on all sides. Sprinkle the meat with 2 tablespoons flour. Stir and add all the marinade. Cook for about 2 hours. Strain the sauce.

Sauté the mushrooms and 1 clove garlic in butter and a little olive oil about 10 minutes. Cook the tagliatelle. Pour on sauce from rabbit and toss. Put tagliatelle in a large serving dish. Surround tagliatelle with pieces of rabbit. Pour mushrooms and their sauce over rabbit and serve.

Region: Valle d'Aosta

Meat Frittata

6 eggs

1/2 onion, chopped

Butter

1/3 pound of any meat, cooked

3/4 cup Parmesan

2 tablespoons parsley, chopped

Salt and pepper

This is a good way to use leftover meat. Grind the meat or chop it finely.

Cook the onion in butter over very low heat. The onion should cook well without browning.

Beat the eggs and add salt and pepper. Add meat, Parmesan and parsley. Add the egg mixture to the onions. Stir the frittata and allow it to cook. The frittata should be a golden color on both sides. Do not allow the frittata to become too hard. The cooked frittata should be rather fluffy and soft.

Region: Lazio

Mixed Roast

Mixed Roast, accompanied by roasted potatoes, is popular in The Marche Region. Just about any combination of meats may be used: pork, beef, chicken, lamb, rabbit.

About 3 kinds of meat, cut into serving pieces

Parsley, chopped

Rosemary, chopped

Garlic, chopped

Salt and pepper to taste

Olive oil

Stock

Put meat pieces in a large bowl. Add parsley, rosemary, garlic, salt and pepper. Drizzle generously with olive oil. Mix well to coat meat with olive oil and seasoning. Cover and allow to rest for at least 1 hour.

Put meat in roasting pan in single layer. Bake at 350º for 1½ hours or until meat is tender and browned. Baste meat with stock and turn from time to time.

S. Pietro - Monte Conero

Meat Pie

1 pound bread dough

⅓ pound calf liver, diced

⅓ pound hog liver, diced

⅓ pound pork loin, diced

1 tablespoon tomato paste

Red pepper flakes

Oregano

Olive oil

Butter

Salt and pepper

Optional: 1 bay leaf

Brown the diced pork in olive oil and butter. Add bay leaf, if using. Cover and cook over low heat for 15 minutes.

Add the two types of liver, salt and pepper. Cook for additional 5 minutes. Add the tomato paste diluted in ½ cup of warm stock or bouillon. Add pepper flakes and oregano. Mix well. Mixture should be moist but not overly fluid. Remove from heat.

Roll out dough to form a pie crust. Divide the rolled dough into two pieces, one larger than the other. With the larger piece, line a buttered pie pan. Cut off excess dough. Pour in the cooked meat mixture and top with the smaller piece of dough. Cut off excess dough and seal, pinching the two pieces of dough together. Bake at 400° for 40 minutes.

For a beautiful presentation, brush the top of the meat pie with beaten egg yolk before baking.

Region: Calabria

Rabbit in Potacchio

Potacchio is a familiar dish to Italian-Americans with roots in The Marche Region of Italy. The distinguishing ingredients of the dish are plenty of garlic and rosemary. Old-timers used vinegar, but modern recipes tend to use dry white wine instead of vinegar. Wine makes a delightful sauce.

1 rabbit, cut into serving pieces

Wine or white vinegar for washing rabbit

2 cups dry white wine or 1 cup white vinegar and 1 cup water

¾ cup olive oil

½ cup finely chopped *pancetta* or bacon

2 cloves garlic, finely chopped

6 cloves garlic, whole

5 or 6 sprigs of rosemary

Allow the rabbit to soak in cool water for 2 or 3 hours. Wash the rabbit with wine or white vinegar.

Put the rabbit in a pot without anything else, and turn the heat to high. Allow the rabbit pieces to dry thoroughly, turning them frequently. Remove the dry rabbit from the pot and clean the pot before moving to the next step.

Put the oil, chopped garlic, chopped bacon and rabbit in the pot. Brown the pieces of rabbit on all sides. Add the whole cloves of garlic, the rosemary and 2 cups of dry white wine or 1 cup white vinegar and 1 cup water.

Cook, covered, over low heat until the meat is tender. Much of the wine/vinegar should have evaporated and the meat should be nicely browned. Remove the cooked rabbit from heat and allow it to rest, covered, for 10 minutes. Move the rabbit to a serving dish, pour on sauce and serve.

Vanda's Stuffed Coniglio

Coniglio is a domesticated rabbit. I watched my cousin Vanda prepare this delicious dish when I visited her in Marina di Montemarciano, Province of Ancona, in July, 1995.

1 large coniglio (rabbit)

Seasoning for *coniglio:*

½ cup diced and browned *pancetta* (or bacon)

2 garlic cloves

½ cup parsley

2 tablespoons rosemary, finely chopped

Salt and pepper

Stuffing:

Coniglio's liver, finely chopped

½ cup Parmesan cheese

1 lb. ground beef, browned

2 cups bread crumbs

3 eggs

Salt and pepper to taste

For browning:

¼ cup *pancetta* (or bacon), finely chopped

1 tablespoons rosemary

2 garlic cloves

Olive oil

Stalk of wild fennel

Open cleaned *coniglio* completely. The opened coniglio should form one flattened piece. Cut off thighs. Mix the seasoning ingredients. Sprinkle salt and pepper on all meat, including thighs. Then spread seasoning mixture over inside of *coniglio* and over thighs. Mix stuffing ingredients. These are not exact quantities but the entire

Oranges of Sorrento

mixture should form into a roll about 1½ inches thick and the length of the *coniglio*. Slightly flatten stuffing roll and place in center of *coniglio*. Then with a large sewing needle and ordinary white sewing thread, sew *coniglio* around stuffing. Sew the legs to the body of the *coniglio*. Cut thighs to form a pocket in each thigh and fill pocket with seasoning as above. Finally, using a heavier cord, tie thighs to *coniglio* and wrap all the meat, *coniglio* and thighs, so that it forms into a roll. In a roasting pan heat all browning ingredients, except fennel, and brown *coniglio*. Remove *coniglio* and line bottom of roasting pan with sticks of wild fennel. Place *coniglio* roll on top of fennel sticks and bake at 350° until done. Cut *coniglio* into serving pieces and slice stuffing. Serve warm.

Burano - Another leaning tower

Burano
4/27/00

Chicken in Potacchio

Chicken, cut into serving pieces

½ cup olive oil or ½ cup salt meat, chopped

1½ cups water

Salt and pepper

1½ cups dry white wine or white vinegar

8 cloves garlic, whole

3 sprigs rosemary

Brown the chicken in olive oil/salt meat. Then add the water. When the water has evaporated, add salt and pepper.

Add the dry white wine or white vinegar, garlic and rosemary. When the chicken is tender, remove rosemary, put chicken on serving platter, pour sauce over the chicken and serve.

Portofino

Assisi - The Hermitage

100 Secondi

A Fun Week Drawing and Painting in Arcevia

It was a fun week drawing and painting with three friends in Arcevia, a hill town about thirty kilometers inland from the Adriatic Coast in Central Italy. We stayed at a house that belongs to my friend Carla Novelli. Like most houses in Arcevia, the house is built into the side of a mountain on levels, according to the slope of the mountain. Carla's house has five levels. Outside the front door, about a hundred steps or more ascend to an upper street level, where we got hot bread and pastries every morning right out of the baker's oven.

After morning coffee, we scattered to different parts of the village carrying our art supplies and portable stools. At noon we met for lunch, which we took turns fixing, and we critiqued one another's morning accomplishments. One day we had lunch at Pinocchio's, a quaint little restaurant in a cave-like setting. It was there I had pasta with figs. The chef, who teaches at the cooking school in Senigallia, said it was an ancient recipe. He said the figs are a special kind that grow locally. I later found an Italian recipe that uses ordinary figs in a pasta sauce (p.29).

In the evenings my friends and I drove to restaurants recommended by locals. We thought the best was La Pianella, high in the mountains above Serra San Quirico. We arrived at the restaurant before serving time. The restaurant owner and his family were eating their dinner at a long table in front of a giant fireplace. Entranced by the food on their table and by the wonderful aromas, we could hardly wait to order. The owner, who appeared to be the chef, asked us to find a table and be seated.

Shortly one of the daughters, a beautiful brunette with sparkling dark eyes, came to take our order for wine and water. We had already decided we wanted the dish that the family had. It looked like a fish with potatoes in a tomato sauce. I thought it was either *baccala* or *stoccafisso* (stockfish). The waitress said it was *Coda di Rospo* (frogfish). She said it was a dish her father had made for the family. It was not on the menu. When the father heard that we were interested in the dish, he brought us a taste of their leftovers. The fish's texture and taste is similar to *stoccafisso* and *baccala*. Stoccafisso is dried cod. Baccala is dried salted cod. They are treated the same in preparation and cooking. In The Marche Region there is a recipe for *Stoccafisso/baccala* that results in a dish very similar in taste and appearance to *the Coda di Rospo* at La Pianella.

We were in Arcevia the night Iraq was bombed. My friends had turned in for the night. I sat on the steps outside our front door to meditate and write:

3-20-03

Arcevia, perched so high in the sky that clouds hover below you, allowing the sun and moon to lighten and brighten your crown, a feel of fantasy, a hint of a world beyond, while hamlets below remain trapped in the gloom of reality.

Tonight bombs of destruction rain down on Baghdad, repeating over and over, over and over again, the damnable devastation of nine-eleven, deeds of insanity we'd prayed never to see again.

Arcevia, may God protect you and keep you as sweet and peaceful, as quiet and safe, as I experience you tonight, the full moon beaming on you so brightly I can read God's inspired word in its light as I sit on the steep ascending steps outside my door at Casa Novelli, and sacred silence is broken only by my neighbor's breathing.

Abandoned Sailboat

Fish

Stoccafisso/Baccala with Potatoes

Stoccafisso (stockfish) is dried cod. *Baccala* is dried salted cod. They are relics of a time when there was no refrigeration for preserving fish. They both require long periods of soaking to soften and, in the case of *baccala*, to remove salt.

2 to 3 pounds *stoccafisso/baccala*, soaked for two days. Change water periodically. Cut into pieces 2 inches wide. Check for bones.

2 tablespoons chopped capers

2 anchovy fillets, chopped

1 celery rib, chopped

1 onion, chopped

1 carrot, chopped

2 cloves garlic, finely chopped

1 tablespoon chopped sage

Salt

Red pepper flakes

½ cup extra virgin olive oil, divided

3 tomatoes, each cut into 8 wedges

3 potatoes, peeled and wedged

½ cup pitted green olives

1 cup dry white wine

3 sprigs rosemary

Mix capers, anchovies, celery, onion, carrot, garlic and sage. Put *stoccafisso* pieces in a roasting pan. Season with salt and red pepper flakes. Drizzle with half the olive oil. Top with half the chopped vegetables and half the tomato wedges.

Spread on the potato wedges. Then spread on the remaining half of the chopped vegetable mixture. Spread on the remaining tomato wedges and the olives. Drizzle with the remaining 1/4 cup olive oil. Pour on wine. Place the rosemary sprigs on top. Bake at 350° for 2 hours.

Stockfish (*Stoccafisso*) in Potacchio

2 pounds stockfish, soaked in water for 2 days, changing water periodically, and cut into serving pieces.

5 cups tomatoes, diced

Red pepper flakes to taste

3 cloves garlic

2 tablespoons chopped rosemary

2 tablespoons chopped parsley

Flour

1½ cups dry white wine

Olive oil

Salt

Heat 3/4 cup olive oil in a large saucepan or tall skillet, preferably stoneware. Add the whole cloves garlic and cook until golden. Remove garlic and add tomatoes, rosemary, parsley and red pepper flakes. Cook for 10 minutes over moderate heat.

Dredge fish in flour. Shake off excess flour. In a second skillet brown fish pieces in olive oil. Add fish to tomato sauce. After 10 minutes, add 1½ cups white wine. Continue cooking covered for 1 to 1½ hours.

Serve from cooking container.

Region: The Marche

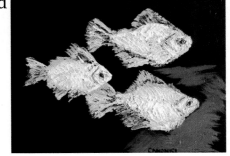

Stockfish (*Stoccafisso*) Messina Style

1½ pounds stockfish, soaked in water for at least 2 days. Change water periodically. Cut into serving pieces.

3 cups tomatoes, diced

3/4 cup green olives, pitted and halved

2 tablespoons capers

1 rib celery, chopped

1 carrot, chopped

1 onion, chopped

1/2 pound potatoes, cut into eighths

1 cup dry white wine

1 tablespoon tomato paste

1/2 cup white raisins, soaked in water

1/2 cup pine nuts

Red pepper flakes to taste

Olive oil

Salt

Flour for dredging

3 or 4 celery leaves

Heat 4 tablespoons olive oil. Add celery, carrot and onion. Cook for 10 minutes over low heat. Dredge fish in flour and brown gently with fried mixture. Add wine and allow it to evaporate. Add tomatoes. Add tomato paste, diluted in sufficient water to cover fish. Bring to a boil and allow to cook, covered, for 30 minutes.

Add potatoes, raisins, pine nuts, salt and red pepper flakes. Cook for 1½ hours over low heat. Add capers and celery leaves. Continue cooking until sauce thickens. At the conclusion of cooking, add olives and drizzle with raw olive oil.

Region: Sicily

Grilled Swordfish

4 swordfish fillets

½ cup olive oil

Pinch of oregano

Salt and pepper

Place the swordfish in a platter or pan, and cover with olive oil seasoned with oregano, salt and pepper. Marinate for 1 hour.

Remove fish from marinade, drain off excess oil and cook on a hot grill 10 minutes on each side. Put the fish on a serving platter. Boil the marinade for 10 or 15 minutes and pour over fish. Serve immediately.

Region: Sicily

Fillets of Trout with a Sour Sauce

4 trout fillets

2 medium onions, thinly sliced

1 clove garlic, finely chopped

1 bay leaf

4 tablespoons white wine vinegar

Olive oil

Salt and pepper

Apply salt and pepper to the trout fillets and brown on both sides in olive oil. When cooked, remove the fillets onto a ceramic dish.

In the remaining oil, cook the onion and garlic. Add the wine vinegar, salt, pepper and bay leaf. Bring to a boil and allow to simmer for 15 minutes. Pour this mixture over the cooked fillets of trout and allow to marinate for about 2 hours.

Place trout on serving dish. Pour onion mixture over fish and serve.

A good accompaniment for this dish is boiled potatoes, sliced and seasoned with salt, chopped parsley and olive oil.

Region: Trentino Alto Adige

Poached Tuna

1½ pounds fresh tuna

1 carrot, cut into large pieces

1 onion, quartered

2 ribs celery, cut into large pieces

1 bay leaf

8 to 10 peppercorns

½ lemon

2 tablespoons chopped parsley

2 or 3 anchovy fillets, finely chopped

1 clove garlic, finely chopped

Juice of 1 lemon

½ cup olive oil

Salt and pepper

In a large saucepan combine carrot, onion, celery, bay leaf, peppercorns, lemon and plenty of salted water. Boil for an hour over medium heat. Remove from heat and allow contents to cool. Strain stock.

Remove skin from tuna and put the fish in the strained stock. Cook until it flakes slightly. Do not overcook. Remove cooked tuna from stock and place it on a serving dish. Combine parsley, anchovies, garlic, lemon juice, olive oil, salt and pepper. Mix well and pour sauce over tuna. Serve immediately.

Region: Calabria

Grilled Tuna

4 slices fresh tuna

1 tablespoon fennel seeds, coarsely ground

3 tablespoons butter

Salt to taste

Press fennel seeds and salt into tuna. Apply olive oil to tuna. Cook on a hot grill or grill pan 6 minutes on each side.

Brodetto (Fish Stew) Ancona Style

Brodetto, a fish stew with a tomato base, is a specialty of The Marche Region of Italy. There are several recipes for *brodetto*, even within The Marche. This recipe belongs to the Province of Ancona. In this recipe, we are using fish available to the southern United States.

2½ to 3 pounds of mixed fish - swordfish, orange roughy, squid, red snapper, shrimp, clams, mussels, lobster. Clean the clams and mussels well and put them into the stew whole. When I make *brodetto* for a large group, I cook the whole lobster in the stew. Then I remove the meat from the tail, chop it and put it in the stew. I put the whole remaining lobster shell on top for presentation.

1 onion, chopped

1 can (28 ounces) tomatoes, pureed or peeled and mashed

3 cloves garlic, finely chopped

1 carrot, chopped

2 celery ribs, chopped

2 bay leaves

1 cup chopped parsley

Red pepper flakes to taste

½ cup white vinegar or 1 cup white wine

Olive oil

Salt and pepper

About 3 cups fish stock (p.65)

6 slices firm bread (one per person)

Cut fish into large pieces. Heat olive oil in a large saucepan, Dutch oven, or preferably, a clay pot. Add onion, garlic, carrot, celery, bay leaves, parsley and red pepper flakes. Cook about 10 minutes or until vegetables are tender.

Add tomatoes and cook about 15 minutes. Then add fish, beginning with the fish that takes the longest to cook. Add pepper and salt. Add vinegar/wine. When wine has evaporated, add fish stock. The amount of fish stock is determined by the amount of liquid in the pot. The brodetto should be very soupy. Cover and cook for 15 minutes.

Toast the bread and place a slice at the bottom of each person's bowl. Ladle *brodetto* over bread and serve immediately.

Some versions of *brodetto* use saffron instead of red pepper flakes and white wine instead of vinegar. Also, I sometimes substitute rice for bread.

Sailing off Senigallia's Velvet Beach

Burano - On the canal

In Venice, Don't Miss Burano

If you go to Venice with a tour group you will probably go to Murano, the island to which all glass furnaces have been relegated, but I doubt you will get to colorful Burano. In Murano you can expect to find nothing but glass. In Burano there's only lace (*merletto*). What I like about Burano are the colorful houses. I've heard two theories to explain why the houses are painted in different bright colors. Some say that because of Burano's remoteness, there's been a lot of inbreeding, resulting in few family names and many people with the same name. For example, there may be ten people with the name Tom Jones. So the Tom Joneses paint their houses different colors and each Tom Jones is identified by the color of his house - Tom Jones in the green house, Tom Jones in the yellow house, and so forth. Another theory holds that women painted their homes certain bright colors so their husbands could find their way home after a night out drinking. I doubt that either explanation is true, but one good reason for continuing to paint Burano's houses in bright colors is to attract tourists.

The island of Burano is quite a distance from St. Mark's. You must allow yourself the better part of a day to go there, but on the way you can stop for a visit at Murano. The principal means of transportation to Burano is the *vaporetto* (water bus). One of the *vaporetto's* stops is The Cemetery, an island to itself. You will not get off there, but you will notice that some of the people who do get off have bouquets of flowers. They're visiting the graves of their beloved dead. Italians honor their dead and take care of their cemeteries.

When I go to Burano, I usually visit the house that's painted checkerboard-style in bright colors. The last time I was there I met the young couple who live in the house. They plan to open the house to the public, like a museum. On Burano I try to see a certain street artist, Juliano Cararo. He's always at the same place, just across the wooden bridge on Burano's main drag. Sometimes he paints in my sketch book. I like to have lunch at *Trattoria da Primo*. The specialty of this restaurant, like all others on the island, is fish. I like the *fritto misto*, fried mixture. On one visit to Primo's I called to the attention of an American friend the eyes of a tiny fish on his plate. The fish looked like a minnow. In a flash my friend put his fork on his plate and refused to eat another bite. In Italy you shouldn't be surprised to find entire shellfish in your soup or pasta.

Because of distance, you would not go to Burano just to have a meal, but when you do go to Burano, plan to have lunch. Be sure to try the fish. It's the island's specialty.

Venice - A View From the Grand Canal

108   Secondi

Contorni-Vegetables and Salads

Venice - vegetable market

Vegetables

Rolls of Asparagus and Ham with Béchamel Sauce

1 bunch of asparagus, about 1½ pounds

½ pound ham, sliced

½ cup grated Parmesan cheese

½ pint heavy cream

Salt

For the béchamel sauce:

2 cups milk

4 tablespoons butter

4 tablespoons all-purpose flour

¼ teaspoon salt

Make the béchamel sauce: Put the milk in a saucepan and heat until milk is almost to a boil. Milk will begin to form a ring of small bubbles.

While milk is heating, put butter in another saucepan and melt over low heat. Gradually add flour to butter and cook about 2 minutes, constantly stirring with a wooden spoon. Remove from heat before flour turns colored.

Very slowly add milk to flour and butter, taking care to stir constantly to completely mix the three ingredients. When all the milk has been added and mixture is smooth, return to low heat and add salt. Stir constantly until sauce is thick. For this recipe, sauce should be very thick.

Add Parmesan to the béchamel sauce.

Tie the asparagus with a string to form one round bunch and cook *al dente* in plenty of salted water. If possible, cook standing in a deep saucepan with hard ends down and tips up. Do not allow asparagus to become limp. Drain the asparagus and cut off the hard ends.

Spread the slices of ham on a board or counter and place 3 or 4 stems of asparagus and a tablespoon of béchamel sauce on each slice. Roll each slice of ham jelly-roll style around asparagus and béchamel. Fasten with a toothpick.

Arrange the rolls in a buttered pan. Pour cream over the rolls and bake at 400° for 15 minutes.

Region: Emilia Romagna

○3   Fields of Sant Angelo

Mario's Beans

Mario Mariani, owner of Ristorante Mario in Rome, is a native of Castelfranco di Sopra, twenty-five kilometers outside of Florence. In 1942 he went to Rome, where he established one of the city's finest restaurants. One of Mario's specialties is beans, which he serves as an *antipasto*. His wife, Maria, also from Castelfranco, does desserts for Mario's.

Mario prides in Tuscan cuisine. He says the secret of his beans is in the cooking method and timing. He recommends using a stoneware pot or a steel pot with a heavy bottom. He starts by putting dried beans into a pot with five times as much water as beans. He adds a clove or two of garlic, depending on the quantity, a stem of sage and a spoonful or two of olive oil. He cooks his beans over very low heat. Mario says that Tuscan peasants cook their beans in smoldering ashes after bread is taken from the *forno* (oven). He does not set a cooking time, which could be as long as four hours. Fresh beans are cooked the same way, but cooking time is less. After the beans are cooked, they are seasoned in different ways.

Beans with Olive Oil

Beans cooked according to Mario's instruction

Olive oil

Salt and pepper

1 or 2 tablespoons of cooking liquid

Combine all ingredients. Vinegar or lemon juice may be added. Beans may serve as an *antipasto* or as an accompaniment for some other dish.

Beans Cooked in a Flask

This dish requires the *zolfino*, a small white Tuscan bean.

1 pound zolfino beans

Sage

2 cloves garlic

Olive oil

Salt and pepper

Mario puts his beans in a large flask filled three-fourths with water. I use a double boiler and put in twice as much water. If additional water is needed during cooking, add hot water. Add salt and sage. Cook over very low heat, taking care that the beans never come to a boil. When the beans are cooked, add extra virgin olive oil, salt and pepper.

Baked Beans

1 pound dried beans, borlotti preferred

3/4 pound tomatoes, peeled and seeds removed

1 leek, chopped

1 or 2 cloves garlic

Small piece of salt meat, cut in strips

4 tablespoons olive oil

Salt and pepper

In a pot or oven pan with cover, combine beans, leek, tomatoes, garlic, salt meat, olive oil, salt and pepper. Add water to cover beans about 2 inches. Cover and bake at 350° for at least 1 hour.

Beans Little Birdie Style

1 pound beans, borlotti preferred, cooked Mario's method (p.111)

½ pound ripe tomatoes, peeled and seeds removed

Stem of sage

2 cloves garlic

Olive oil

Salt and pepper

Sauté garlic and sage in olive oil until garlic is lightly golden. Add tomatoes. Slowly mix in the cooked beans. Add salt and pepper. Bring to a gentle boil and cook 15 minutes.

Gargoyle in the flower garden

Eggplant Baked in Tomato Sauce

3 medium eggplants

2 cups basic tomato sauce (p.16)

¼ cup chopped basil

¼ cup chopped parsley

2 cloves garlic, minced

Olive oil

Salt and pepper

Cut eggplants in half lengthwise. Salt the open sides and place the halves on an incline for an hour to dispose of bitter liquid.

Wash eggplant halves and score the open sides. Place halves in a baking dish, open side upward.

Spread mixture of chopped basil, parsley and garlic over eggplant halves. Apply salt and pepper to taste. Spread tomato sauce over eggplant halves and drizzle generously with olive oil. Bake at 400° for 45 minutes to 1 hour or until eggplants are tender. Cover halfway through baking.

Region: Sardinia

Fried Eggplant Balls

2 pounds medium eggplant

3 eggs, separated

2 cups bread crumbs

2 cups grated Pecorino cheese

½ cup chopped basil

Red pepper flakes to taste

Salt and pepper to taste

Vegetable oil for frying

Cut eggplants into small pieces, put in colander, salt well, and allow to rest at least 1 hour to remove excess fluid. Dry, removing salt and fluid.

Cook in salted water, but be aware eggplant already has some salt.

Drain eggplant and chop finely. Combine eggplant with bread crumbs, Pecorino cheese, egg yolks, basil, red pepper flakes and pepper.

Form eggplant mixture into balls the size of Ping-Pong balls. Fry in hot oil. The eggplant balls may be dredged in egg whites and bread crumbs and then fried.

Region: Calabria

Marinated Fried Eggplant

3 eggplants
3 cloves garlic, thinly sliced
3 bay leaves
15 peppercorns
Salt
Vinegar to barely cover eggplant slices

Slice eggplants lengthwise, eliminating first and last slice. Fry eggplant slices in plenty of boiling vegetable oil.

Place eggplant slices on paper towels to remove excess oil. Salt to taste. Place slices in a ceramic container. Spread sliced garlic over slices and add bay leaves, peppercorns and vinegar. Allow marinated eggplant to rest overnight.

The marinated eggplant will be preserved and last for several days. Serve either as an *antipasto* or as an accompaniment to meat.

Region: Calabria

Cinque Terre - Manarola

Cinque Terre - Manarola at dusk

Eggplant Parmesan

The original Sicilian recipe for Eggplant Parmesan included sliced potatoes and sliced onion, each fried separately and placed in alternate layers with the eggplants. Finally, there was a topping of tomato sauce, medallions of mozzarella and basil leaves.

3 medium eggplants

1 quart basic tomato sauce

½ pound sliced mozzarella

2 cups grated Parmesan

Bread crumbs

Butter

Vegetable oil for frying

Cut the eggplants lengthwise and allow them to drain by either laying them out in the sun or by salting and laying them on an inclined surface.

Fry the eggplant slices in plenty of hot oil. Place the cooked slices on paper towels to drain off excess oil. In an oiled pan, layer the eggplant slices, tomato sauce, mozzarella slices, and Parmesan cheese. End with a topping of Parmesan, bread crumbs, and small pieces of butter.

Bake at 400º for 30 minutes. Remove from oven and allow to rest for 5 minutes. Garnish with fresh basil.

Region: Sicily

114   Contorni

Eggplant Piccante

3 medium eggplants

2 cloves garlic, minced

1 teaspoon dried oregano

1 teaspoon red pepper flakes

¾ cup olive oil

2 tablespoons mild white vinegar

Salt

Slice the eggplants, apply salt and place slices on an inclined surface to drain off fluid. Put eggplant slices in salted boiling water a few at a time and cook for 5 minutes. Remove slices from boiling water onto a clean cloth or paper towel.

In a small bowl mix 2 or 3 pinches of salt, white vinegar, olive oil, chopped garlic, red pepper flakes and dried oregano. Stir well to mix ingredients.

Arrange the dried eggplant slices in a pan and pour on seasoned oil. Allow eggplant slices to marinate for a day or two before serving.

Region: Calabria

A glimpse of Florence

Eggplant Slices, Tomatoes and Mozzarella

2 or 3 medium round eggplants

Flour for dredging

4 round tomatoes, sliced

2 anchovy fillets, chopped

2 cloves garlic, finely chopped

Sliced mozzarella

½ cup basil, chopped

Vegetable oil

Olive oil

1 teaspoon white vinegar

Salt and pepper to taste

Slice eggplants. Dredge eggplant slices in flour and fry in plenty of vegetable oil. Do not allow to get too crisp. Remove eggplant slices from oil and place on paper towels to drain.

Oil a baking dish and place in 1 slice of eggplant at a time. On each slice of eggplant place a slice of tomato and a thin slice of mozzarella. Place the next slice of eggplant halfway over the previous slice and continue process until bottom of dish is covered. The eggplant slices should be so staggered that half of the previous slice is exposed. Bake at 400° for 10 minutes.

In a saucepan heat ½ cup olive oil. Add finely chopped anchovies, garlic, basil, vinegar, salt and pepper. Stir well to dissolve anchovies. Remove from heat.

Remove eggplant slices from oven and immediately pour on sauce. Allow to cool slightly. Eggplant may also be served cold.

Region: Campania

Early morning shopping

Stuffed Eggplant

3 round eggplants

1½ cups bread crumbs

1 cup milk

¾ cup pancetta or lean bacon, diced

½ pound ground beef

2 cloves garlic, chopped

¾ cup dry white wine

2 cups stock

1 small can diced tomatoes

Olive oil

4 tablespoons butter, divided

Parsley, chopped

Basil, chopped

1 tablespoon chopped capers

Salt and pepper to taste

Pinch of nutmeg

Grated Parmesan

Cook pancetta/bacon and garlic in 2 tablespoons butter. Add meat and stir well. Add wine and cook over high heat until wine has evaporated. Add salt, pepper, nutmeg, tomatoes and warm stock. Cook over low heat for an hour or longer, adding stock or milk as necessary to maintain a dense, fluid consistency. This is the sauce.

Cut the eggplants in half and carve out about two-thirds of the pulp. Chop the pulp and cook with parsley and basil in the remaining 2 tablespoons butter and some olive oil. Add salt and pepper and capers.

Moisten the bread crumbs with milk. Squeeze out excess milk and add to eggplant pulp. Add ¾ cup Parmesan cheese and the eggs. Mix well. Fill cavity of eggplants with this pulp mixture.

Put the stuffed eggplants in a baking dish. Cover with meat sauce and plenty of Parmesan. Bake at 400º for 45 minutes or until eggplant shells are cooked.

Large zucchini may be prepared in the same manner.

Region: Puglia

Senigallia - The Velvet Beach

Venice - gondolas and San Giorgio

Marinated Boiled Eggplant

2 eggplants, cut in thick slices

12 basil leaves

1 clove garlic

1 tablespoon vinegar

2 tablespoons olive oil

Salt to taste

Salt the eggplant slices, place them on a slanted surface and allow them to drain for 20 minutes or longer.

Put 2 or 3 inches of water in a wide pan, add salt and bring to a boil. Dry eggplant slices with a cloth or paper towel and place them in the boiling water for 15 minutes. Drain the eggplant slices, allow them to cool and place on a platter.

Mash together the garlic, basil and salt to form a paste. Add the vinegar and oil. Mix well and pour over eggplants.

Caponata

2 pounds eggplant, preferably long and seedless

Salt

Olive oil

2 cups coarsely chopped celery, white interior part

1 onion, chopped

1 small can tomato paste

3 teaspoons sugar

1 cup good quality red wine vinegar

2 tablespoons capers, chopped

¾ cup green olives, chopped

Pepper to taste

Salt to taste

Dice eggplant, sprinkle with salt and place in a colander to drain for at least 1 hour. Dry eggplant with paper towel and fry in plenty of hot oil until well browned. Remove eggplant from oil and spread on paper towels to drain.

Fry celery in same oil until tender and drain on paper towels.

Pour about ¼ cup of the same oil into another pan and cook onion until lightly golden. Dilute the tomato paste in ½ cup warm water and stir into onion. Season with salt and cook 15 minutes over moderate heat. Add sugar, vinegar, capers, olives, eggplant and celery. Add plenty of freshly ground pepper and salt to taste. Simmer 10 minutes. Serve cold.

Sautéed Mushrooms

Mushrooms, cleaned with damp cloth and sliced

Olive oil

Garlic, minced

Parsley, chopped

Thyme, fresh or dried

Lemon juice, just enough to season

Salt and pepper

Heat olive oil in skillet. Add mushrooms and sauté over medium heat until tender. Add garlic and cook about a minute or two longer.

Add parsley, thyme, lemon juice, salt and pepper. Stir and serve.

Florence - shops on Ponte Vecchio

Baked Onions

1 large onion for each person

Olive oil

Bread crumbs

Sage, finely chopped if fresh, or dried, sufficient to season bread crumbs

Salt and pepper

Cut a little off the bottom of peeled onions to keep them from rolling over. Cut about ½ inch off the top. Arrange onions in a baking pan. Pour a little olive oil on top of each onion. Bake at 350° for 1 hour or until onions are tender.

While onions are baking, heat additional olive oil in a skillet. Add bread crumbs and sage. Cook over low heat, stirring constantly, until crumbs are lightly golden. Season with salt and pepper.

When onions are cooked, remove from baking pan. Add crumbs to pan and stir them around to soak up pan juices. Remove moistened crumbs from pan. Put onions back in pan. Spoon bread crumbs on top of each onion. Return onions to oven and bake 5 minutes longer.

Serve warm or at room temperature. Drizzle on a little olive oil before serving.

SORRENTO

Steamed Broccoli with Garlic and Olive Oil

Broccoli, in quantity desired, trimmed and cut lengthwise into serving-size pieces

Olive oil, sufficient to coat broccoli

2 or 3 cloves thinly sliced garlic, depending on quantity of broccoli

Salt and pepper to taste

Lemon wedges for garnish

Steam broccoli until tender but not mushy.

Heat oil in a skillet. Add thinly sliced garlic and cook until very lightly golden. Arrange broccoli in serving dish. Sprinkle with salt and pepper. Drizzle with oil and garlic.

Garnish with lemon wedges. Serve immediately.

*Green beans and pole beans with garlic and olive oil can be prepared and served in the same way as broccoli.

Zucchini in Tomato Sauce

4 medium zucchini, sliced

1 small can diced tomatoes

1 onion, chopped

Olive oil

Salt

Pepper

Oregano

Cook the onion in a saucepan until lightly golden. Add tomatoes and salt to taste. Cook over medium heat for about 10 minutes.

Add the zucchini, pepper and a pinch of dried oregano. Check for salt and add more if needed. Continue cooking for about 20 minutes.

Pour zucchini into a serving dish and serve.

Region: The Marche

Senigallia - beach changing booths

Sunset on the Adriatic

Baked Zucchini with Tomatoes

1 onion, sliced

3 tablespoons olive oil

4 medium zucchini, cut into ½ inch slices

1 garlic clove, minced

1 teaspoon fresh oregano or ½ teaspoon dried

Salt and pepper to taste

1 can (14 ounces) diced tomatoes or 2 cups fresh tomatoes coarsely chopped

1 teaspoon orange zest

In a skillet sauté onion till lightly golden. Arrange zucchini slices in a baking pan. Pour sautéed onions and oil over zucchini. Add garlic, oregano, salt and pepper.

Bake in a preheated oven at 400° for 10 minutes. Then add tomatoes and orange zest and continue cooking until tomatoes form a thick sauce, about 20 minutes.

Serve hot or at room temperature.

Marinated Zucchini

1 pound zucchini

Olive oil

¼ cup vinegar

1 clove garlic, chopped

1 tablespoon mint, chopped

Salt

Slice zucchini lengthwise and spread the slices on paper towels to dry for about 1 hour. Fry zucchini slices in hot oil until lightly browned on both sides.

Spread zucchini slices in a deep dish. Cover the zucchini with some of the oil used for cooking, the vinegar and some raw oil.

Sprinkle with salt, chopped garlic and mint leaves. Allow zucchini to rest for 2 or 3 hours before serving.

Region: Puglia

Fried Zucchini

Zucchini, desired quantity

Flour for dredging

Vegetable oil for frying

Salt and pepper

Cut zucchini into four pieces and slice each piece lengthwise into pencil-size pieces. Put zucchini pieces in a colander, sprinkle generously with salt and allow to rest at least 1 hour.

Dry zucchini well with paper towels. Season with pepper and dredge lightly through flour. Fry zucchini until crisp in plenty of vegetable oil.

Region: Emilia Romagna

Roasted Potatoes

Roasted potatoes are delicious with assorted meat roasts. They look so good and give a great aroma to the whole house.

Potatoes, scrubbed and cut into small wedges

Olive oil, just enough to coat potatoes

Garlic, minced

Rosemary, minced (dried will work but use half as much)

Salt and pepper

Put potatoes in a bowl and season with olive oil, garlic, rosemary, salt and pepper. Stir well to coat potatoes with seasoning. Transfer potatoes to a baking pan and arrange in a single layer.

Bake, uncovered, at 400º for 1 hour, or until potatoes are browned and crisp. Turn once or twice during cooking.

Sliced potatoes may be used. Parsley may be used instead of rosemary.

Potato and Cheese Casserole

2 pounds potatoes

¼ pound Parmesan cheese

4 tablespoons butter

1 cup heavy cream

Salt and pepper to taste

Boil potatoes with skin for 30 minutes. Drain, skin and slice potatoes. Line the bottom of a buttered casserole dish with slices of potatoes. Spread thinly sliced pieces of Parmesan and dots of butter over potatoes.

Repeat layering process ending with cheese and butter. Then pour cream lightly over all and bake at 400˚ for 30 minutes.

Region: Emilia Romagna

Stuffed Tomatoes

4 round tomatoes

3 cups cooked rice

1 cup diced mozzarella

1 cup green peas, cooked in salt water

1 cup diced ham

1 cup grated Pecorino or Parmesan

Salt and pepper to taste

½ cup olive oil

Cut off and reserve the top of each tomato. With a small spoon, scoop most of the pulp from the tomatoes. Combine the tomato pulp, rice, mozzarella, green peas, Pecorino, olive oil, salt and pepper. Mix well.

Lightly salt the inside of each tomato and fill each tomato with rice mixture. Replace the tops on tomatoes.

Bake tomatoes at 400º for 30 minutes or until tomatoes are cooked.

Region: Sicily

Venice, Santa Maria della Salute

Stuffed Cabbage

1 curly leaf cabbage (verza) (Use one large leaf or two smaller leaves for each portion.)

½ pound ground pork

½ pound ground beef

Salt and pepper

2 cloves garlic, minced

½ cup chopped parsley

Olive oil for frying

Butter for frying

1 onion, chopped

1 egg

1 cup bread crumbs

1 cup stock

Parmesan cheese

Wash the cabbage leaves and put them in boiling water for 1 minute. Remove the leaves and spread them on paper towels or a cloth to dry.

Mix the meats with salt and pepper to taste. In a saucepan heat oil and cook onion until lightly golden. Mix in meat and cook until nicely browned. Finally mix in garlic and parsley. Remove from heat and allow meat mixture to cool. Stir in egg and bread crumbs. Place a large spoonful of meat mixture on each cabbage leaf. Roll the leaves around the meat and tie with a string. Fry the cabbage rolls in olive oil and butter for 10 minutes. Brown both sides. Add a cup of stock, cover, and cook over low heat until hot. Allow the rolls to cook over moderately high heat until golden.

Remove the string from rolls and serve with the sauce from cooking container. Sprinkle with Parmesan cheese.

Region: Friuli Venezia Giulia

Stuffed Peppers Diavolo

6 peppers, red and yellow

8 to 10 fillets of anchovy, chopped

2 tablespoons capers, chopped

1½ cups chopped black olives

2 large ripe tomatoes, chopped

2 cups cubed hard bread

1 cup bread crumbs

2 cloves garlic, minced

½ cup chopped parsley

Roast peppers quickly over grill or under broiler. Peel peppers. Cut a slit down the side of the pepper and clean inside.

Place peppers in a baking pan. Put a few drops of oil at bottom of each pepper and sprinkle inside and outside with bread crumbs.

Toast the bread cubes in a skillet with a little olive oil and place a few cubes in each pepper. Also put in some chopped tomato, a little chopped anchovy, some chopped olives, a little chopped capers and some chopped garlic and parsley. Drizzle olive oil over filling. Close the pepper and fasten with toothpick. Drizzle well with olive oil. Bake at 400° for 30 minutes.

This dish may be prepared with peppers that are not roasted and peeled. In such a case bake 45 minutes to 1 hour.

Region: Campania

Stuffed Peppers Piccante

4 peppers

1 cup bread crumbs

1 cup black olives, chopped

1 cup grated Pecorino cheese (or Parmesan)

6 anchovy fillets

½ cup chopped parsley

1 tablespoon chopped capers

1 tablespoon pine nuts

Olive oil

Salt and pepper to taste

Optional: Soaked raisins

Heat four tablespoons of olive oil in a skillet. Add bread crumbs and stir constantly with a wooden spoon until bread crumbs are well toasted. Remove bread crumbs from heat and add chopped olives, Pecorino, anchovies, parsley, capers, pine nuts, salt and pepper. Stir in ½ cup olive oil and mix well.

Clean peppers and cut them in fourths. Fill each piece with mixture. Place the stuffed peppers in a baking dish and drizzle with olive oil. Bake at 300° for 45 minutes to 1 hour.

Soaked raisins may also be added to the filling.

Rome - The Forum

Roasted Peppers and Garlic

Equal amounts of green, red and yellow peppers, cut into wedges

1 or 2 onions, cut in wedges

8 whole garlic cloves (quantity of onion & garlic depends on quantity of peppers)

Olive oil

Parsley, chopped

Juice of 1 lemon or vinegar of choice

A little thyme

Salt and pepper

Lemon wedges for garnish

In a baking dish combine peppers, onion and garlic cloves. Drizzle with olive oil.

Roast vegetables at 400°, turning every 15 minutes until peppers, onions and garlic are golden, about 45 minutes.

Toss cooked vegetables with chopped parsley, lemon juice, thyme, salt and pepper. Arrange in serving dish and garnish with lemon wedges.

Serve warm or at room temperature.

Peppers Stuffed with Potato and Egg

4 yellow peppers, cut in halves lengthwise (Leave stem on one half of each pepper)

2 red peppers, cut into strips lengthwise

1 onion, chopped

4 small potatoes, boiled, peeled and cubed

6 eggs

4 tomatoes, peeled, seeds removed, cut into strips

1 or 2 tablespoons butter

3 or 4 tablespoons olive oil

Salt and pepper

3 tablespoons Parmesan

Heat 3 or 4 tablespoons olive oil in a skillet. Add onion and cook until lightly golden. Add red peppers, tomatoes, salt and pepper. Cook over low heat for about 30 minutes.

Beat eggs with a pinch of salt. Melt butter in another skillet. Add eggs and stir with a wooden spoon over very low heat until eggs are lightly set. Remove from heat. Add potatoes and the Parmesan cheese. Add pepper and salt.

Fill the halved yellow peppers with mixture. Pour tomato and pepper sauce over top. Bake at 350° for 20 minutes or until peppers are cooked. Serve two halves on individual warm plates. Garnish with a piece of fresh herb.

Venice - Chiesa San Giacometo di Rialto

Peperonata

The Italian word for bell pepper is *peperone*. *Peperonata* is a bell pepper mixture. Farm families sometimes placed a pot of *peperonata* in the center of the family table and spooned it onto slices of bread or polenta that was fried, baked or grilled. It was also used with poached eggs and as an accompaniment to meat. The *peperonata* is also good as a pasta sauce.

3 tablespoons olive oil

1 large onion, sliced thinly

1 clove garlic, sliced thinly

4 red, yellow or green peppers, cut in strips

Oregano (fresh-1 tablespoon; dry-1 teaspoon)

1 bay leaf, crumbled

1½ cups tomatoes, diced, or 1 can (14 ounces) tomatoes

Heat the oil and add onion, garlic, oregano and bay leaf. Stir and cook about 5 minutes, till onions are lightly golden. Add peppers, salt and pepper. Turn heat to high and cook about 10 minutes.

Add tomatoes, reduce heat and cook until tomato juices are reduced, about 15 minutes.

Wilted Greens with Olive Oil and Garlic

Italians eat a lot of cooked greens, various kinds of greens. It is not uncommon to see ladies gathering wild greens in open fields. When I was a child, I helped my mother gather dandelions for salads.

This recipe can be used with any type of greens: Swiss chard, spinach, mustard greens, lettuce.

Greens

Olive oil

Garlic, minced

Salt and pepper or red pepper flakes

There are at least two ways to cook the greens. First you may steam the greens. Cook until they are wilted but still green.

The other way I have cooked the greens is in a covered pot with minimal water. Wash the greens and put them in a pot without drying. Water attached to the leaves should be sufficient. If you think there is not enough water, add a little to the bottom of the pot. Cover and cook over moderate heat. Stir so greens will wilt evenly. Again, cook until wilted but still green.

Heat oil and garlic in a skillet. Add greens, salt and pepper or red pepper flakes. Toss until heated through.

Greens with Sausage and Wine

Olive oil

Garlic, minced

Sausage, without casing and crumbled

Wine, about a cup, depending on quantity of greens and sausage

Greens, cooked (p.127)

Salt and pepper or red pepper flakes to taste

Heat olive oil. Add garlic and cook till lightly golden. Add sausage and brown. Add wine and cook until wine has evaporated. Add cooked greens, salt and pepper or pepper flakes, and heat through.

Drizzle with additional olive oil and serve immediately.

Venice - Murano lighthouse

Grilled Vegetables

For the marinade:

Olive oil

Oregano, minced

Garlic, minced

Salt and pepper

Just about any vegetable in season:

Peppers, red, yellow or green, cut into wedges

Onions, red or white, cut into thick slices or wedges

Whole mushrooms, stemmed

Zucchini, sliced lengthwise

Eggplants, sliced

Yellow squash, sliced lengthwise

Mix olive oil, oregano, garlic, salt and pepper for the marinade.

Arrange vegetables in a single layer on a platter and pour on marinade. Allow vegetables to rest in marinade for about 1 hour at room temperature.

For grilling vegetables, it is best to use a grilling pan or basket to keep vegetables from falling through onto flames. Grill vegetables until browned on both sides, about 10 minutes. Arrange grilled vegetables in serving dish and drizzle with additional olive oil. Garnish with lemon wedges.

Grilled vegetables may be served hot or at room temperature.

Vegetable Pie

For filling:

3 pounds seasonal vegetables (eggplants, potatoes, carrots, green peas, zucchini, onions)

4 tablespoons olive oil

Salt and pepper

For crust:

4 cups flour

1½ cups Crisco

Salt

For the filling, chop vegetables. Heat oil and half-cook vegetables. Add salt and pepper.

To make the crust, mix flour, Crisco, a pinch of salt, and a little warm water. Work the dough until it is soft and elastic. Break the dough into two pieces, one a little larger than the other. Stretch the two pieces by hand and with a rolling pin.

Oil a large pie or tart pan. Use two pans if necessary. Line pan with the larger piece of dough. Pour in vegetables. Cover with smaller piece of dough. Trim off excess dough and seal edges by pinching. Design the top with a spiked wheel cookie cutter, pressing lightly. Make a small cut in the center to allow steam to escape. Bake at 350° for about 1 hour. Serve hot or at room temperature.

Region: Sardinia

Potato Frittata

The frittata is one of the most versatile and certainly one of the simplest Italian dishes. The only ingredients necessary are eggs and just about any vegetable or meat. The frittata is an excellent way to use leftovers.

If vegetables or meats are precooked, chop and mix with 5 or 6 eggs, depending on quantity desired. Heat an oiled skillet and pour in mixture. If vegetables and meats are raw, chop them and cook in a little oil. Scramble the eggs, pour into skillet with cooked ingredients, add salt and pepper, and stir well. Cook over moderate heat until the frittata is set and golden on both sides. You may finish the frittata by placing it in a warm oven for a few minutes.

In our home we sometimes had potato frittata for breakfast.

1½ cups diced potatoes

¼ onion, finely chopped

6 eggs

Salt and pepper

Mix all ingredients. Heat an oiled skillet. Pour in mixture and cook until golden on both sides.

Temple of Segesta Sicily

CANONIC

Exploring Sicily

My latest trip to Sicily was with six friends, traveling in a nine-passenger van. The size of our van was especially noticeable when somewhere between Cefalu and Palermo, we made an emergency exit into a small village in search of gasoline. The streets were narrow. Locals leaned out of windows to peer at the rare sight, outsiders in a monstrous vehicle. Backhoes laying water lines backed out of the way to let us by. Several times we asked for directions to a gasoline station and repeatedly were told to go down to the *campo sportive* (athletic field). One man told us we could not get to the gasoline station, but we could borrow a can from the station attendant. Confused about gasoline at an athletic field and the necessity of a can, we finally found the field and understood. The highway we were traveling from Cefalu to Palermo is on the south side of town, while the highway going in the opposite direction is on the north side. The gasoline station is on the north side, opposite the direction we were traveling. We parked on the edge of the athletic field just behind the gasoline station and two of us made our way through a forced opening in the cyclone fence that separates the field from the station. We borrowed a can, got our gasoline and zigzagged back to the westbound highway to Palermo.

Four of our traveling companions flew home from Palermo. Robert Canizaro and I continued our travels through Sicily in a smaller, more manageable vehicle. Robert's grandfather, Giuseppe Cannizzaro[1], left his home in Poggioreale, Sicily, when he was fifteen and, like so many Sicilian immigrants to the South, made his way to New Orleans. Our visit to Poggioreale was one of my most interesting Sicilian experiences.

There are two Poggioreales, an old and a new, just a few kilometers apart, located in Sicily's Belice Valley, 67 kilometers inland from Trapani. In 1968 an earthquake destroyed the old Poggioreale and several other towns in the Belice Valley. Robert's cousin, Leonardo, gave us a tour of old Poggioreale, now in ruins and abandoned. Its stone and brick streets are overgrown with weeds. It was early evening when we were there and already bats were circling overhead. The abandoned ruins gave the impression of a ghost town. We saw the collapsed theatre, the standing façade of a gutted church and the belfry of another church. I took pictures of Robert and Leonardo in front of the ruins that used to be their great-grandfather Giacomo Cannizzaro's home. It was a touching moment for Robert.

We slowly wandered amidst the crumbled houses sharing our impressions and feelings quietly, almost in whispers, as if not to disturb the silence of a sacred place. At the end of the bricked path that was once Poggioreale's main street, we looked down on fertile fields adorned with olive trees, corn and vegetables. Outside Old Poggioreale there was life.

Suddenly the silence of the abandoned town was broken by the sound of bells and tromping hoofs. A herd of sheep spurred on by two dogs came running down the slope of a side street. A rugged-looking shepherd followed. He stopped to chat with us. Leonardo knew him. The shepherd's name was Felice. His weather-worn face was a portrait of simplicity, sincerity, kindness and years

[1]The spelling was changed to Canizaro in the United States

Felice - the Sicilian shepherd

of hard work. I took pictures and later attempted to paint Felice's face, but it was not the same as seeing the shepherd in person and in context.

Later that afternoon we visited new Poggioreale, which, to me, has a plastic look. The design, color and building materials seem not to fit in with Sicily's Greek temples and overall antiquity. I got the feeling that locals liked their old town better. In the old town their living quarters mingled in with their shops, business places and churches.

When I visit interesting places, I like to pick up something to take home. In Poggioreale I got the recipe for Cousin Lina's pasta with eggplant and swordfish (p.32). Robert made notes about Cousin Vito's fruit orchard.

Salads

The Classic Salad

The Classic Italian salad is simple:

Salad greens

Salt

Vinegar

Olive oil

The classic salad, like so many Italian dishes, is surrounded by ritual. It is served after the main course because it helps digestion. Salt, vinegar and oil are passed around and individuals dress their own salad. This allows each person at table to apply salt to taste. Some choose not to use vinegar on salad.

Certain salads are served as *antipasti* and the Italian cook's imagination is allowed free reign in his or her creation.

Four Tomato Salads:

Any gardener knows that tomatoes tend to ripen all at the same time. In the Region of Campania, where vegetables are plentiful, housewives serve tomatoes in various forms. These four tomato salads use few ingredients, but each salad is somewhat different. Ingredients for the four salads are:

Tomatoes

Mozzarella

Anchovy fillets

Black olives

Celery

Tuna in oil

Garlic

Basil

Oregano

Salt and pepper

Olive oil

Salad with Tomatoes, Black Olives and Mozzarella

Cut tomatoes into small wedges and mix with 1/2 cup pitted black olives, diced mozzarella and a few leaves of basil, broken by hand. Season with salt and drizzle with olive oil. Toss and serve.

Tomato and Crouton Salad

To make croutons: Cut hard bread into cubes and toast in a skillet with olive oil.

Cut tomatoes into small wedges and put into a serving bowl. Add salt and pepper. Drizzle with extra virgin olive oil and add croutons, a few leaves of fresh basil and 2 or 3 whole cloves of garlic. Toss and serve. The garlic is just for aroma. It should not be served to your guests.

Salad with Tomato, Mozzarella and Anchovy

Cut tomatoes into small wedges and put into a serving bowl with diced mozzarella and chopped anchovies. Season with a little oregano, salt and pepper. Drizzle with olive oil, toss and serve.

Salad with Tomatoes, Celery and Tuna

Cut tomatoes into small wedges. Coarsely chop a cup of celery, using only the inside white part. Combine tomatoes, celery, a half-cup of pitted olives, a can of tuna in oil, and a few leaves of basil. Season with salt and pepper. Drizzle with extra virgin olive oil. Toss and serve.

Cucumber Salad

Medium cucumbers, in desired quantity

1 cup heavy cream

1/2 lemon or 1 teaspoon white vinegar

Pinch of paprika

Salt and pepper

Peel and slice cucumbers. Salt the cucumbers and spread them in a single layer on paper towels. Allow to drain for at least 1 hour.

Lightly beat heavy cream with a teaspoon of white vinegar or the juice of 1/2 lemon, salt, pepper and a pinch of paprika.

Dry cucumber slices and put them into a serving bowl. Pour cream sauce over cucumbers and sprinkle lightly with paprika.

Region: Trentino Alto Adige

Caprese (Tomato and Mozzarella)

Tomatoes, sliced

Fresh mozzarella, sliced (same number of slices as tomatoes)

Basil, chopped

Salt and pepper

Olive oil

Place tomato slices on a serving dish. Place a slice of mozzarella on each slice of tomato. Season with salt and pepper. Sprinkle with basil. Drizzle with olive oil.

Marina's Seafood Salad

Marina Calderigi and I are two generations apart. Her maternal grandmother, now deceased, was my cousin. We are also separated by thousands of miles and vast oceans. Marina lives in Ancona on the Adriatic Sea and I live in Mississippi. Although we're separated by generations and space, Marina is the Italian relative I communicate with most. We like so many of the same things: The Marche Region's countryside, the old abandoned Italian farmhouses, wading barefoot in the Adriatic, and sometimes we talk about the differences that a hundred years have brought about in the Italians of her world and mine.

Marina does not consider herself a good cook. I think she sells herself short, because she compares herself with her mother, Anna Maria, who is among the best. On one occasion when I was staying a few days with Marina and her husband, Alessio, her mother asked Marina what she planned to feed me. Marina answered, "Whatever we eat." Her mother, with a typical Italian expression, looked to the heavens, put her hands to her head and exclaimed "*O, Dio Mio*" (Oh, Dear Lord). Nonetheless, Marina always puts out great meals. She doesn't spend long hours in the kitchen like her mother and she doesn't

Assisi - Street scene

fret about presentation; but I always leave her table with fresh cooking ideas. On my most recent visit at Marina's table, she had this refreshing seafood salad.

Calamari and/or squid

Canned chunk tuna

Olives, chopped

Carrots, shredded

Capers

Hard-cooked eggs, chopped

Olive oil

Lemon juice

Salt and pepper

Mayonnaise or Dijon mustard

For quantities use personal taste as a guide.

Boil calamari and/or squid with 1 carrot, 1 onion, 1 teaspoon red pepper flakes and 2 ribs celery until tender. Discard vegetables. Cut calamari and/or squid into small pieces.

Combine calamari and/or squid, tuna, eggs, carrots and capers. Season with lemon juice, salt and pepper. Sprinkle with olive oil and toss. Add mayonnaise or mustard and toss again.

Prepare a day ahead to allow flavors to penetrate.

Bread and Tomato Salad (*Panzanella*)

In olden times *panzanella* consisted of thick slices of firm bread, sometimes toasted, rubbed with a clove of garlic and seasoned with salt, pepper, olive oil and vinegar. It served as an afternoon snack (*merenda*) for farm families working in fields. Now *panzanella* is a delicacy that serves either as an *antipasto* or as a salad.

Firm bread, preferably at least a day old

Fresh tomatoes (equal to amount of bread), coarsely chopped

½ cup onion (for 4 cups tomatoes), finely chopped

½ cup celery (for 4 cups tomatoes), finely chopped

Basil

Olive oil

Red wine vinegar

Salt and pepper

Soak bread in water and squeeze out excess. Bread should be moist.

In a bowl mix tomatoes, onion, celery and basil. Season with olive oil, vinegar, salt and pepper. Mix well. Olives, cucumbers, onion, and other ingredients may be added. Break bread into bite-size pieces and spread it over the bottom of a serving dish. Sprinkle with salt, pepper and basil. Drizzle lightly with oil.

Spread tomatoes evenly over bread.

Florence - a collage

Dolci-Desserts

Florence - Ponte S. Trinita from Ponte Vecchio

The fine pastries for which Italians are known are seldom used as the dessert (*dolce*) at the end of a meal. They are used for the morning *espresso* break or the *merenda* in late afternoon. The most common conclusion to a good meal is fresh fruit and cheese (*frutta e formaggio*). The *macedonia*, similar to a fruit cocktail, is a favorite. In recent years, *gelato*, the Italian ice cream, has come into use as a dessert, especially in restaurants, and also *granita*, a coarse, frozen ice similar to sherbet. Generally, treats served at the end of meals are less sweet than American desserts.

Pears Baked with Honey

4 large pears, halved and cored with a spoon to form boat-shaped opening

2 tablespoons butter

2 tablespoons lemon juice

4 tablespoons honey

1 teaspoon lemon zest

¼ teaspoon nutmeg

4 tablespoons plain yogurt

Arrange pears, cut side up, in a baking pan. Place a piece of butter in each pear half. Drizzle pears with lemon juice and honey. Sprinkle with lemon zest and nutmeg.

Bake at 350° for 40 minutes or until pears are golden. Serve hot or at room temperature. Top each pear half with 1 tablespoon yogurt.

A bouquet for Graziella

An Italian Lady & an American Beverage

My friends, Livio and Graziella Cingolani, live in Senigallia, Province of Ancona. Livio is retired from city maintenance. Graziella is a sweater maker, a *magliaia*. She has worked with some of Italy's finest designers. Italian women retain their maiden names, consequently the name Pegoli, Graziella's maiden name, is attached to her sweaters, except those made for specific designers.

Graziella's grandfather, Rafaele, purchased a small plot of land across the street from Senigallia's north beach. He had a small house there, about an acre vineyard and a garden. Eventually that plot of land was passed on to Graziella and it became the first of the Cingolani's several properties.

Livio and Graziella built a two-story house on Rafaele's land. The upper level was where Graziella's mother lived until she died. The Cingolanis now have several apartments, which they rent to beachgoers during midsummer. Four of the apartments are on their beach property. Others are in the City of Senigallia.

On my visits I usually stay in one of the beach apartments because I like to get around by bike. Senigallia is flat, ideal for biking, and residents take advantage of the convenience of biking, no difficulty parking and no fuel expense. On any given day you can see men and women going to work or running errands by bike. Women do their morning shopping and old men get to their chatting spots by bike.

The Cingolani's latest grand project was the restoration of a three-story villa located on a 15-acre plot in the Sant Angelo area, about five miles inland from Senigallia and the Adriatic Sea. Looking downward northeast from the villa there's a grand view of Senigallia and the Adriatic. Looking southeast you can see the small house where Graziella grew up. In her early teenage years she rode her bike every day down the sloping pebble covered road to Senigallia, where she studied sweater-making from the nuns. If you look upward to the west, toward the village of Sant Angelo, you see the belfry of the little church where Graziella and Livio were married. Is there any wonder that Graziella has a passionate attachment to the restored villa?

Livio and Graziella use the villa as a house in the country and from time to time they host Americans I recommend. My friends love the villa, the panorama, the olive trees, the cherries, the big green figs and the cool sea breeze year round.

In late May and early June, 2004, I traveled Italy with Charles and Regina Burckel and their fifteen-year-old granddaughter, Ashley. We started at Cinque Terre and then went to Florence and Rome. In Rome we picked up a car and made our way up to Senigallia by way of Spoletto, Deruta, Assisi and Gubbio. We arrived at the Cingolani Villa one evening about dinnertime. It had been a hard day. In fact, we had experienced two or three hard days on our drive from Rome to Senigallia. In Spoletto we lost a taillight. In Assisi we encountered a fender-bender. And at Fano, after a curvy mountainous drive through the Apennines and just before entering the Autostrada to Senigallia, the car died. Thank God for cell phones. I got in touch with my relative Marina and she arranged for us to be picked up and taken to Rimini, where we got another car. The villa and the Cingolanis were welcome sights.

Graziella had dinner ready, but Charles asked for a few minutes to relax. We had stopped at the supermarket to stock up on refreshment supplies. Charles made martinis for all of us, including Livio and Graziella. In the typical Italian way, Graziella downed her drink and took a second. Dinner was delayed but Graziella was "happy." She gave me a hug and exclaimed, "I have so much fun when your friends come."

Two years have passed since my trip with Charles and Regina, and since then the Cingolanis have converted one of their beach apartments into a bar for summer beachgoers. An Italian bar is not a bar in the American sense. Their bars do have some light alcoholic beverages, but they are more like coffee and ice cream shops, with pastries, light snacks and soft drinks. Italians have wine at all meals but breakfast, but they don't know hard liquor, except for grappa in the cool Alpine country.

Graziella called me recently to say that she had opened her bar, called Bar Rafaele, after her grandfather, who purchased the beachside property. A young lady was to come to train as a waitress, but in the meantime Graziella was having a ball visiting with beachgoers she's come to know over the years. In the course of our telephone conversation, Graziella asked, "Do you remember the drink your friend fixed for me, the one I liked so much, the one with the olive?" I told her I would call Charles for the recipe. The next day I gave Graziella the recipe for Vodka Martinis: Fill a 9-ounce, Old-Fashion glass with chipped ice. Pour vodka over ice until glass is almost full. Add a teaspoon of juice from the olive jar. Finally, add a twist of lemon and mix. Add one or two olives on a toothpick.

Charles gave me the recipe for another drink that I called in to Graziella. I told Graziella she should call the first drink "Big Moose," that's what we call Charles, and she should call the latter "Regina": Fill a 12-ounce highball glass half full with ice. Add about 1½ ounces of gin and 1 tablespoon of maraschino cherry juice. Fill the glass with 7-Up or Sprite. Squeeze in one-quarter of a lemon and leave lemon in glass. Mix or shake well and garnish with a maraschino cherry.

I told Graziella she should serve the drinks sparingly. Like most Italians, she is not familiar with hard liquor. My hope is that she will serve her newly found American drinks with care, or her guests will be rolling in the sand.

There are three things that Graziella likes to fix: her Nut Sauce Pasta (p.25), her Stracciatella (p. 65), and her Biscotti (p.141). Ordinarily she uses walnuts for the sauce. They're native to Italy; but she has used pecans that I bring from Mississippi. She and Livio have two small pecan trees that they have grown from Mississippi pecans, but the pecan trees seem not to do very well in their soil and climate.

Piazza Roma Senigallia   Canonica

Graziella's Biscotti

1½ cups chopped almonds

3 envelopes yeast, dissolved in a little water with a teaspoon of vinegar

4 eggs

All-purpose flour as needed for proper consistency

1 full cup sugar

½ teaspoon vanilla

Combine eggs, sugar and yeast. Add flour until a thick consistency is formed. Add chopped almonds and work dough a little, adjusting for flour or water as needed for proper consistency. Dough should be pliable but not sticky.

Divide dough into four or five parts. From each part of dough make a roll about ¾-inch thick and about 12 or 14 inches long. Arrange rolls on greased cookie sheet and bake in preheated oven at 350º for about 30 or 40 minutes, until golden brown.

Remove rolls from oven and allow to cool. Cut rolls on a slant into 2-inch pieces. Arrange pieces on cookie sheets on their cut side. Bake additional 10 minutes in preheated oven.

Enjoy a taste of Italy.

Carrot Tart

½ pound carrots, peeled

½ pound almonds, without hulls

5 eggs, divided

1 cup sugar

1 tablespoon rum

Zest of 1 lemon

1 cup bread crumbs, toasted in skillet with butter

Butter

Grind carrots and almonds in food processor. Try not to grind too finely. Grind with 2 or 3 quick pulses.

Beat egg yolks with sugar. Add the carrots, almonds, lemon zest, rum and bread crumbs. Mix well.

Beat egg whites until they peak and fold into carrot mixture. Pour entire mixture into buttered tart or pie pan and bake at 400° for 30 or 40 minutes

Allow the tart to cool before serving.

The Adriatic - Three Umbrellas

The following three desserts are prepared by Maria herself at Ristorante Mario, Rome

Pumpkin Tart

For two or three tarts:

3 cups cooked butternut squash or some other sweet squash such as the Japanese Kabocha

2 cups apple (1 apple), peeled and very thinly sliced

1 cup white raisins

6 tablespoons butter, melted

6 eggs

¾ cup sugar (or Splenda)

¾ cup liqueur (Amaretto, Frangelico, brandy, rum)

Pinch of cinnamon

1 envelope active dry yeast

1 cup apricot marmalade

Flour, about 1 cup or less

Cut the squash in half, remove seeds and boil in big pot with a little water, skin side down. Boiling water should not cover the meat of the squash. Squash may be baked. Cook until tender.

Combine the meat from the squash, apples, raisins, butter, eggs, sugar, liqueur, cinnamon, marmalade and yeast. Sprinkle a little flour at a time while stirring, until flour is throughout the mixture.

Butter three shallow pie pans. Pour in mixture to thickness of about ½ inch. Tarts should be thin. Bake at 400° for 40 minutes. May be sprinkled with powdered sugar when tarts are removed from oven.

Rome
Spanish
Steps

Canova

Apple Tart

For 2 tarts:

4 apples, peeled and very thinly sliced

3 eggs

6 tablespoons sugar (or Splenda)

8 tablespoons (1 stick) butter

½ cup liqueur. Maria uses an Italian liqueur, *Alchermes*. Frangelico and Amaretto will work.

1 envelope dry active yeast

Flour, 1 cup or less

Mix all ingredients except flour. Then sprinkle flour a little at a time, while stirring, until the ingredients come together, but the mixture should not be very dense or hard.

Pour into buttered pans to thickness of about ½ inch. Bake at 400° for about 30 to 40 minutes. While tart is still warm, garnish with thin slices of apple and sprinkle with powdered sugar. The tart may be served at room temperature.

Ricotta Tart

For 2 tarts:

3 cups (30 ounces) ricotta

¾ cup liqueur of choice. I use Frangelico or Amaretto. Maria uses an Italian liqueur, *Alchermes*.

½ cup sugar (or Splenda)

Dough for pie shells

Mix first three ingredients together and pour into pie shells to a thickness of ½ inch. If fresh dough is used for pie shells, be sure to butter pans. Bake at 400° for 20 to 30 minutes. Powdered sugar may be sprinkled on before serving.

Zabaione (Egg Custard)

For 4 servings:

8 egg yolks

8 heaping tablespoons sugar

½ cup Marsala

Beat the egg yolks well to a froth. Add the sugar and gradually add the Marsala.

Put in a double boiler and stir constantly until dense. Do not permit the mixture to boil.

Remove from heat and serve, hot or cold, with biscotti.

Tiramisu (translation: "Lift me up")

- 9 eggs, separated
- 9 tablespoons sugar
- 1 cup brandy or sweet Marsala, divided
- 1 cup strong espresso coffee, divided
- 1 pound mascarpone cheese at room temperature, divided
- 2 pints heavy cream
- 2 packages Savoiardi or ladyfingers
- 4 tablespoons grated semisweet cocoa, divided

Make a *zabaione* by beating the egg yolks and add sugar gradually in the top of a double boiler until ivory colored. Add ¾ cup brandy and whisk over simmering water until mixture begins to thicken. Let cool.

Stir ½ cup espresso coffee into the mascarpone. Whip heavy cream to soft peaks. Beat egg whites until stiff. Fold the egg whites into the *zabaione*.

Arrange Savoiardi (ladyfingers) in a single layer in the bottom and on sides of large trifle bowl (10 or 11 inches) or rectangular dish (10 x 7 x 3). Sprinkle Savoiardi (ladyfingers), until soaked but not soggy, with mixture of the remaining brandy and espresso (½ of each).

Over the Savoiardi (ladyfingers), layer half the mascarpone, then half the *zabaione* and one-third of the whipped cream. Sprinkle with one-third of the cocoa. Repeat layers, finishing with remaining whipped cream and sprinkle with remaining cocoa. Refrigerate at least 2 hours, preferably overnight. Serves 12 to 15.

Venice - Murano
6-13-04

Ciambelle

This is a hard holiday sweet bread, delicious with coffee or wine. I got this recipe from Cecilia Sandroni Cuicchi, a lifelong friend from Shaw. The recipe was brought to America by Cecilia's grandmother a hundred years ago.

6 large eggs (7 medium)

6 teaspoons sugar

6 teaspoons oil

2 teaspoons lemon extract

¼ cup whiskey

¼ teaspoon baking powder

¼ teaspoon baking soda

4½ cups sifted bread flour

Icing:

½ cup water

1 cup sugar

1 egg white, beaten

½ teaspoon lemon extract

Nonpareils

Beat eggs and add sugar, oil, lemon extract, whiskey, baking powder, baking soda and flour. Mix well and knead on a floured board until dough is smooth. Cut dough into 16 or 18 equal pieces.

On a floured board, roll each piece into a 4-inch roll. Set on an oiled board until all are rolled.

In a large pot, three-fourths full of boiling water, drop 6 rolls in and when they float to the top, boil for another 2 to 3 minutes. Drain on a wire rack and place on a dry towel. Repeat for the remaining rolls.

Ciambelle needs to be baked twice.

First baking: Place about 8 rolls on a cookie sheet, allowing space for expansion. Bake in 500º oven for 15 minutes. Lower heat to 400º; bake for an additional 15 minutes. Lower heat to 350º and bake for another 15 minutes. If the rolls are a nice golden color at 400º, you may bake them at 300º for the last 15 minutes. Let cool on rack. Repeat for remaining rolls.

Second baking: Preheat the oven to 500º, and bake for 10 minutes.

Let rolls dry a day or so before icing. Boil water and sugar until it spins a thread. Pour slowly over 1 beaten egg white. Mix until thick enough to spread. Add lemon extract. Brush icing on Ciambelle and sprinkle with nonpareils.

Sorrento

Panettone

This is a sweet bread, a specialty for Christmas. This recipe came from my dear friend, Teresa Cuicchi Malatesta, who has researched Italian families in the Mississippi Delta.

1 package dry yeast

1 cup warm water

1 egg

¾ cup chopped citron

¼ cup Crisco

3 cups sifted flour

1 teaspoon salt

¼ cup sugar

Dissolve yeast in water; add all other ingredients except flour and citron and mix well. Then add flour and citron. Knead well and let rise in a warm place for about 1½ hours. Knead again on a floured board. Place in a greased tube pan and let rise for a while.

Bake at 375° for 35 to 45 minutes until brown.

Anise Cookies

3 cups all-purpose flour

3 eggs

1 tablespoon baking powder

¾ cup sugar

¼ teaspoon anise flavoring

1 stick butter

1 cup chopped pecans

Juice of 1 orange

Zest of 1 orange

Raisins (optional)

Whiskey (optional)

Mix all ingredients and knead slightly. Gradually add more flour until dough consistency is hard.

Make dough into ⅓ to ½-inch rolls and cut into 2-inch pieces.

Place cookies on a baking sheet about 1 inch apart. Bake at 400° for 20 minutes or until golden brown.

My sister-in-law, Louise, got this recipe from my sister Nancy Mancini Biondini.

Riomaggiore- Cinque Terre

My Brother Joe's *Castagniole*

Castagniole is a fried pastry made during *carnevale*, carnival time, before the beginning of Lent. Joe and his wife, Louise, put this recipe together from information they gleaned from our parents and other old-timers. The ingredients are similar to a recipe I got from my Italian relative Ondina. The difference is that Ondina's *Castagniole* are more or less ball-shaped. Joe makes his *Castagniole* flat and cuts them into angular shapes. Whether round or flat, the cooked *Castagniole* should puff.

2¼ **cups flour**

4 **tablespoons sugar**

4 **eggs**

3 **tablespoons vegetable oil**

1½ **tablespoons vanilla extract or lemon extract**

½ **teaspoon salt**

¼ **teaspoon baking powder**

Mix flour with baking powder and put aside. Mix together all other ingredients.

Put flour mixture in a bowl. Make a well in the flour and pour in other ingredients. Work into a dough. Work dough until smooth and velvety. Make dough into a ball, wrap in a cloth and let rest 30 minutes.

Roll dough into a sheet. Cut into irregular shapes about 3 x 5 inches, more or less. Fry over medium heat in plenty of vegetable oil. Remove *Castagniole* to paper towels to drain and cool.

They may be sprinkled with powdered sugar. We prefer them without the sugar.

Giuliana's *Ciambelline*

Elaine Trigiani got this old Loro Ciuffenna[1] recipe from her friend Giuliana who had been using butter and oil to make the cookie. Elaine reverted to the original recipe using only oil. Her friend preferred the "all oil" version and she now makes them that way herself. The recipe makes 70-75 cookies.

2.2 **pounds flour**

Scant ½ cup sugar (more for dipping)

1⅓ **cup olive oil**

1 **cup Vin Santo (or Marsala or any wine, white or red)**

4 **teaspoons baking powder**

Pour the flour onto a work surface and make a large wide well. Into the well pour the olive oil and Vin Santo, the sugar and then the baking powder. Mix with a fork slowly incorporating flour until the dough comes together and you can work it with your hands. Work in as much flour as necessary until the dough is smooth, soft and elastic leaving aside the extra flour. Knead the dough for a few minutes until the ingredients are well mixed.

To shape the cookies, cut the dough into chunks more or less the size of a walnut, roll each one on the work surface with your palm, forming a length of dough and join the ends to make a little ring (*ciambellina*) 2½ – 3 inches in diameter. Dip the formed cookies in sugar to coat one side and place them, sugar side up, on a cookie sheet.

Bake the cookies at 420° for about 20 minutes, until they are golden brown and slide freely on the cookie sheet. Remove them from the pan and cool on a wire rack.

In the Florentine tradition, *ciambelline* are accompanied by a glass of Vin Santo in which the cookies are dipped.

[1] Loro Ciuffenna is a Tuscan village about 45 km southeast of Florence

Florence - Borgo Penti 15

148 Dolci

Limoncello

5 lemons

2½ cups vodka

2½ cups sugar

2 cups water

Remove zest from the lemons and discard the inner white pith. Put the zest in a jar and pour the vodka over the top. Cover and let stand in the sun for 8 days.

Prepare a syrup with the sugar and water. Bring to a boil in a saucepan. Cook for 10 minutes to make a syrup. Put the syrup aside to cool.

Filter the vodka and lemon liquid and pour it back into the jar. Stir in the sugar syrup. Allow the *limoncello* to rest for 15 days.

Latugi

The recipe for *Latugi* was passed down in the Bassi family from Edith Malavasi Bassi Brawner. Edith Malavasi grew up in the vicinity of Rosedale, Mississippi. Her family was among the Italians of Mantuan origin who settled on the Scott Plantation north of Rosedale. When Edith was sixteen years old she married Giulio Bassi whose family had also settled on the Scott Plantation. After Giulio's tragic death from a robber's gunshot, Edith married Mr. Brawner. The name "*Latugi*" is undoubtedly Italian-American with origin in the Mantuan dialect. *Latugi* are very similar to fried pastries found in other regions of Italy.

4 tablespoons sugar

4 eggs

3 tablespoons olive oil

¼ teaspoon baking powder

½ teaspoon salt

1½ tablespoons vanilla

2¼ cups plain flour

1 qt. corn oil for frying (Mazola)

Mix sugar, eggs and the 3 tablespoons oil. Beat well. Add other ingredients. Knead on a floured board until smooth (approx. 10 – 15 minutes). Dough will be very elastic. Roll dough until very thin (approx. 27 inches in diameter).

Cut into 1 ½ x 2 inch rectangles. Cut five slits in each. Pull two opposite corners through second slit on each end forming a pretzel effect. Drop into hot oil and deep fry until golden brown. Sprinkle with powdered sugar while hot.

Yields: 80

Venice - Burano

Marzocca- at Via Garibaldi

Sauces
For General Use

Portofino

Béchamel Sauce (White Sauce)

2 tablespoons butter

2 tablespoons flour

2 cups milk

Salt and pepper to taste

Pinch of nutmeg

Heat butter in saucepan. Add flour to melted butter and whisk until blended.

In another saucepan bring milk to a boil. Add milk to flour, stirring rapidly to blend. Cook over low heat for 15 minutes.

This recipe will result in a medium consistency. For a thinner sauce, use 1 tablespoon each of butter and flour. For a thicker sauce, use 3 tablespoons of butter and flour.

Gremolata Sauce

½ cup grated lemon peel

2 teaspoons minced garlic

3 tablespoons parsley

2 tablespoons olive oil

Salt and pepper to taste

Mix all ingredients together. Gremolata is good with meats and fish. It can be added to meat or fish at the end of the cooking period.

S. Margherita

Temple of Minerva –
Assisi

Canonica

Marsala Sauce

½ cup dry Marsala

1 clove garlic, chopped

3 cups stock, preferably veal

1 tablespoon butter

Salt and pepper to taste

Heat Marsala, garlic and pepper, and cook until Marsala is reduced by two-thirds. Add stock and salt and cook for an additional 2 minutes.

Strain sauce, add butter and mix. Serve hot on chicken or meats.

Pesto Sauce

3 cups basil leaves

2 cloves minced garlic

1 cup olive oil

1 tablespoon pine nuts

Salt to taste

½ cup Parmesan or Pecorino cheese

The original way to make pesto was to use a mortar and pestle. I use a food processor. Grind all ingredients, adding sufficient oil to form a dense, flowing sauce.

Many Italian recipes add a little parsley to pesto. Sometimes a little anchovy is added. Two or three tablespoons of lemon zest gives the pesto a special citrus taste that is especially good with fish.

Venice, San Giorgio

Pinzimonio

This simple sauce is common in all regions of Italy. In The Marche Region it is called *cazzimperio*. It is used for dipping raw vegetables, especially in summer. In our home, we used the sauce for dipping radishes and celery sticks. Some American restaurants mix this sauce at table for dipping bread. They call it "Italian butter."

Olive oil

Salt

Pepper

Lemon juice (optional)

Simply mix the ingredients together.

Mayonnaise

Beat well one egg yolk, a pinch of salt and a pinch of white pepper. Continue beating, gradually adding a little olive oil. As soon as the mixture starts to become dense, add a few drops of lemon juice or white vinegar. Continue adding oil alternately with lemon juice, and beat until all the ingredients form a dense mixture.

Garlic Sauce

Prepare the same way as for mayonnaise, except add 3 cloves of well crushed garlic to the egg in the beginning. This sauce is used with meat, fish and vegetables.

Salsa Verde (Green Sauce)

2 tablespoons capers

3 anchovy fillets

2 cloves garlic, minced

½ cup parsley, very finely chopped

Olive oil

White vinegar

Juice of 1 lemon

Black pepper or cayenne pepper to taste

With mortar and pestle or in food processor, grind capers, anchovy fillets and garlic. Mix with chopped parsley and dilute with oil, vinegar and lemon juice. Add black or cayenne pepper. Brush this sauce on meat, fish and vegetables.

Senigallia - Chiesa di Immacolata

Adriatic Fishing Camp

Tips for Cooking

Riviera del Conero

Tips for Cooking Italian

Al dente - Pasta is always cooked *al dente,* which means that it is not cooked until mushy. Pasta should have a slight bite but not taste raw.

Basil - can be chopped or broken and used in larger pieces. Unless basil is obviously dirty, it is cleaned with a damp cloth without washing.

Bread crumbs - are used in many Italian recipes. The best bread crumbs are those made in your own home. Put old, hard bread in a food processor and grind well. You may freeze extra bread crumbs in a plastic bag.

Bouillons - All stocks are available in the form of bouillon. For the average recipe, bouillon works very well for making stock in a hurry.

Capers and anchovies - preserved in salt should be washed well before use. If capers are large, they should be chopped.

Cloves - Using cloves stuck into whole onions to season stocks is a practice that originated in Piedmont, which borders with France. It is a French influence.

Cooking pasta - When cooking pasta it is not necessary to put oil in the water.

Eggplant - is usually sliced, salted and allowed to rest on a slanted surface for 45 minutes to an hour to drain away bitter water. Sometimes a heavy object,

Snow in the mountains

such as a big plate, is placed on the eggplant to force the water out. Wipe the eggplant or wash it before cooking.

Fish - are plentiful in Italy, because the country is almost surrounded by water; but the types of fish are different from ours in the United States. Consequently, I have included just a few fish recipes in this book.

Garlic - is sliced, minced, crushed or used whole. An easy way to peel garlic is to crush it with the handle or blade of a knife. After a slight crush, the hull comes right off. If the garlic is to be removed after the oil or sauce is seasoned, use the whole clove or large pieces.

Garlic powder - Never use garlic powder or garlic salt. A genuine Italian recipe will never specify garlic powder or garlic salt. You can always tell when a cook uses them instead of fresh garlic. The garlic in garlic salt keeps coming up long after you've finished your delicious meal.

Ham and *prosciutto* - come from the same part of the hog. Italians call ham *prosciutto cotto* (cooked prosciutto) and they call regular prosciutto *prosciutto crudo* (raw prosciutto). In this book we distinguish by simply calling one "ham" and the other "prosciutto."

Herbs - Use half as much dried herbs as you would use fresh. Put dried herbs in at the beginning of the cooking process, fresh herbs at the end.

Herbs and spices - are sometimes tied together in cheesecloth and put into the sauce in the form of a little package or bundle, a *mazzetto di odori* (a little bunch of herbs).

Mushrooms - are cleaned with a damp cloth without washing.

Oil - generally refers to extra virgin olive oil. However, vegetable oil is most often used for deep frying. When a recipe asks for olive oil, it is understood that the meaning is extra virgin olive oil. The first time I saw an olive oil mill at work, I vowed never to use any olive oil except extra virgin. After the first pressing of the olives, the remains -- like hulls, pits and trash -- are carried by belt to a location outside the mill, where they form a pile on the ground. A machine like a backhoe loads the olive remains onto a truck that takes them to a mill at another location, where chemicals are added to help extract any oil left after the first pressing. The result is regular olive oil.

Sant Angelo - Olive Trees

Gondolas at rest

Oil Temperature - Test the temperature of oil by flicking very little flour into the oil. If the oil boils violently, it is hot enough to obtain a crisp, golden crust.

Onion - Choice of onion is determined by the taste you want. Red onion is sweet and may be used when raw onion is required. Yellow onion is a good all-purpose onion, but too strong to serve raw; cooked, it is sweet. White onion is less sweet and more pungent than yellow. Shallots have a more subtle flavor than onions.

Quantities and measurements - are general in Italian recipes. An Italian recipe may refer to a *manciata* (a handful), a *pizzico* (a pinch or dash), a *ciuffo* (a tuft) of parsley. When it comes to quantities, Italian recipes leave much leeway to the taste and imagination of the cook.

Parsley - always refers to flat-leaf parsley. It is generally added at the conclusion of the cooking process.

Panna - is an Italian cooking cream used in many Italian sauces. When *panna* is not available, I substitute heavy cream. It is not uncommon to use *panna* and tomatoes together.

Pepper, black - is always freshly ground. Consequently when a recipe requires pepper, it is understood that it is asking for freshly ground black pepper. Occasionally an Italian recipe will ask for peppercorns, particularly in stocks and certain soups.

Pepper, Hot - Hot red pepper is called *peperoncino*. Most often the hot pepper, *peperoncino*, is cut into three or four pieces and used to season the olive oil at the beginning of the cooking process. It is allowed to fry in the oil briefly and then removed before other ingredients are added. Be sure to cut the hot pepper or it will explode. In my home I prefer to use red pepper flakes instead of the whole *peperoncino*.

Pepper, Roasted - Recipes sometimes require peppers to be roasted and peeled. To roast a pepper put it under the broiler or over the grill and allow the skin to turn black or dark brown all over. Then put the pepper in a paper bag to cool. After the pepper has cooled, peel off the outside skin, remove the stem and clean out the inside. Do not wash the roasted pepper in water. The roasted pepper is oily. Be sure to place the pepper on a cookie sheet or a piece of foil if it is to be roasted under the broiler.

Rice, How to Cook - In a saucepan, put one cup of rice, two cups of water, a tablespoon of butter or olive oil, and salt to taste (about a teaspoon). Bring to a boil. Cover and turn heat to low. Cook until all water is absorbed, about 20 minutes. Rice should be cooked. Test, and if rice is not done, add a little boiling water and cook until all water is absorbed. Allow rice to rest, covered, for 5 or 10 minutes. I sometimes use a bouillon cube instead of salt.

Sauces - are usually used sparingly on pastas, barely coating the pasta. In this book, recipes generally assume that you are cooking one pound of pasta. Most of the sauce recipes will make more sauce than you will need for one pound of pasta. The extra sauce may be served on the side for those who prefer more, or the extra sauce may be frozen for future use.

Sauces, tomato - become bitter and acidic when they cook too long. Good sauces don't have to cook all day. The sweetest are those that cook in less than an hour. To avoid a bitter and acidic sauce, use chopped carrot in the starter, not sugar.

Sauces, meat - are enriched by bones. My mother used the chicken's feet, neck and head to season her tomato sauce. If she had beef or pork bones, she used them. Cook the bones until they are well browned before adding other ingredients.

Sausage - When an Italian recipe calls for sausage, the meaning is "Italian sausage."

Scarpetta - In informal settings you may wipe the good pasta sauce from your dish with a piece of bread. This is called "making a *scarpetta* (a little shoe)." In other words, you make a little shoe to scoop good sauce from your dish. The *scarpetta* should not be done at formal meals. In an informal setting the cook may consider the gesture a compliment.

Shellfish - are most often used in a recipe without removing the shell. Thus clams and mussels are frequently left whole in a sauce, as are scampi.

Soffritto - refers to the fried mixture of oil, herbs and vegetables at the start of a sauce or any cooking process. For example, you may begin a pasta sauce by heating your oil and frying a chopped mixture of onions, celery and carrot.

Spaghetti, how to eat - Do not break spaghetti before cooking, and do not cut spaghetti for eating. Spaghetti is sold the right length, about 10 inches. Serve spaghetti in a shallow bowl with a rim, like a shallow soup bowl. Make a little space toward the front of your dish by pushing the spaghetti toward the center of the dish with your fork. This allows you a little space for working your fork. Moving your fork clockwise, wrap a little spaghetti around your fork. Do not try to wrap too much at one time. If you notice that you have too much spaghetti around your fork, put it back on the plate and start over.

Stock, extra - (broth) can be frozen for future use. Try freezing stock in ice trays. Store cubes in plastic bags. When you need stock, take out the amount you need.

Stock, fish - is made in the same way as meat stock, but use the throw-away parts of fish instead of meat.

Stock, meat - is made by boiling the meat or bones with an onion, celery, carrot and parsley. I prefer to season stock with salt and pepper at the time of use.

Stock, vegetable - is made by using the vegetables without meat or fish. Use more vegetables and less water.

Sticking - To avoid sticking heat your pan over moderate heat before starting, even before adding oil.

Tomatoes - for sauces are usually peeled and seeded. Italians usually use tomatoes in the form of a puree that is obtained after the tomato is strained to remove skin and seeds. Tomato in this form is called *passato*. Vegetable purees are also called *passato*. If you do not want a puree, peel the tomato by dipping it in boiling water. The skin will remove easily. Squeeze the tomato slightly to remove the seeds.

Trito - Herbs used for a sauce most often are minced all together. A recipe may ask for a *trito* (a chopping) or a minced mixture of garlic, rosemary, parsley and basil. A *trito* can include any herb. The most common combination consists of garlic and parsley.

Water - Do not run water through your cooked pasta unless you intend to use the pasta in a cold salad.

Wine - Good wine is a common ingredient in Italian cuisine. Italian cooks use wines they like to drink. If a wine is not fit for drinking, it is not fit as a cooking ingredient.

Venice - Rialto bridge

Selected Sources

Port of Senigallia - Fishing boat

Bianco, Mulino. Ricette Tradizionali Sulla Tavola. Parma, Italy. Barilla G. & R. Filli, 1986.

Biondi, Lisa. Cucina Regionale Italiana: 365 Ricette. Roma: Legatoria del Sud Ariccia, 1992.

Biondi, Lisa. Il Meglio della Cucina Traditionale. Novara, Italy: Stampa Officina Grafiche de Agostini, 1998.

Boni, Ada. Italian Regional Cooking. New York: Bonanza Books, MCMLXIX.

Borgognoni, Libby (Compiled by). Old World Cookery: Italian and European Favorites. Lake Village, Arkansas: Our Lady of the Lake Altar Society: 1990.

Buonassisi, Vincenzo. Spaghetti in 150 Modi. Ideazione e Realizzaione Anna Condemi. Le Guide di Anna.

Consolata, Sister Germana. Sister Germana's Cookbook. New York: Catholic Book Publishing Co., 1988.

Corriere Della Sera. La Grande Cucina Regionale. Milano, Italy. Rizzoli Libri Illustrati, 2005.

Del Conte, Anna. Italian Kitchen: Gli Antipasti. New York: Simon and Schuster, 1993.

Field, Carol. In Nonna's Kitchen. New York: Harper Collins Publishers, Inc., 1997.

Hazan, Marcella. Essentials of Classic Italian Cooking. New York: Alfred A. Knopf, 1992.

Istituto Geografico DeAgostini. Cucina Rapida. Torino: 1991.

Kasper, Lynne Rossetto. The Splendid Table. New York: William Morrow and Company, Inc., 1992.

La Buona Tavola, Mensile di Cucina, a Cura Ersilia Canesi, Ambrosio Turati, Nunzia Monanna, Laura Renaldini. A monthly bulletin on Italian Regional Cooking. July, 1983 – July, 1984.

La Cucina Tirolese, Fourth edition, 1989. Editor: Unione Albergatori e Publici Esercenti (So. Coop. A.R.L.) Consorzio S.R.I. e Gruppi Secializzati delle Aziende Gastronomiche ed Alberghiere del Tirolo.

Marchesi, Gualtiero. La Cucina Regionale Italiana (no. 1-12). Verona, Italy: Editore, Arnoldo Modadori.

Morresi, Nicola Mazzara. La Cucina Marchigiana. Ancona, Italia: Industrie Grafiche Filli Aniballi, 1978.

Palla, Monica. Primi: 100 Ricette. Milano, Italy. De Vecchi Editore, 2005.

Palla, Monica. Secondi: 100 Ricette. Milano, Italy. De Vecchi Editore, 2006.

Palla, Monica. Verdure: 100 Ricette. Milano: De Vecchi Editore, 2005.

Panzini, Senigalia, Notes on Marche foods and cooking from the cooking school, Istituto Professionale di Stato, A Panzini.

Riolo, Claudio. Pescato e Cucinato, IL Pesce Quotidiano, dal Pescatori Alla Tavola. Azzurro Comme il Mare, Commune di Senigalia, Marche, 2005.

Roggero, Saverina. 365 Insalate. Roma: Legatoria de sud Ariccia, 1998.

Ruggiero, Anna Marie. The Roseto Cuisine Cookbook: A Century in Transition. 1993.

Sheldon, John, Pamela. Risotto. New York: Williams-Sonoma, Simon and Schuster, 2002.

The Silver Spoon, published in English by Phaidon Press Limited. New York, 2005. First published in Italian by Editoriale Domus as Il Cucchiaio di Argento, 1950.

Simmons, Marie. Italian Light Cooking. New York: The Putnam Publishing Group, 1992.

Spagnol, Elena. Cucina Super Veloce, 200 Ricette in 10 Menuti, 1986, Sperling & Kupfer Editori, S.P.A., Le Guide di Grazia.

Index of Recipes

Port of Senigallia

Porto di Senigallia
5-15-02

Contorni (Vegetables and Salads)

Rome, Pantheon

Venice - St. Mark Basilica

The sweetness you bring to God's Creation is special and no one dares take it away, not even death itself.
Paul Canonici